thank you Jesus *for the* french fries

CHAD D. STARY

FREILING
PUBLISHING

First Paperback Edition

Some names, businesses, places, events, locales, incidents, and identifying details inside this book have been changed to protect the privacy of individuals.

Published by Freiling Publishing,
a division of Freiling Agency, LLC.

P.O. Box 1264
Warrenton, VA 20188

www.FreilingPublishing.com

PB ISBN: 978-1-956267-71-6
eBook ISBN: 978-1-956267-72-3

Printed in the United States of America

Contents

Foreword

THIS BOOK IS a selection of over 15 years of weekly "thoughts" written to focus on the importance of daily life and business principles. The title *Thank you Jesus for the French Fries* starts with the true meaning of being *thankful* and knowing all things come at a price. Growing up, getting to eat out was rare and a treat. Most times getting a hamburger meant bringing it home to then pull chips out of the cabinet and pour tea. I must note that we never missed a full home cooked meal, as every evening my mom would bring her kitchen magic. Thank you, Mom, for all those meals when I know you were tired after a day's work. I also want to thank my grandfather and my dad for always praying and saying thanks for each meal which continues with our family today. Both also gave me a strong work ethic and ensured a provision was made to always have a full table.

Having not taken for granted a hamburger, when my only daughter Melyn was old enough to take out to eat, I would teach her the *thankful* lesson. She would say what she wanted and once we all sat down I would say, "Melyn, who do we thank for this?" and she would say, "Jesus, Daddy." I wanted her to know even in the smallest things like ordering *French Fries*, there is a time to reflect and be grateful. It was Melyn's strong encouragement and dream that this book was published.

1

"There are those rare days when your past influences walk back into your life."

THERE ARE DAYS that really make you think more about life than other days. This Saturday was one of those rarities. Early Saturday morning, I waited for the sun to give me enough daylight to get started. I had a call that covered a lot of good ground. Then to work—knocking out the list of things to do—I was under the clock to meet the equipment dealer before noon. So the list was getting done on time and then it was in the truck with the trailer headed to Shiner Tractor. I arrived on time and met the owner who had his guys working on the shredder. As I agreed to take it, he said, "We need to replace one more bearing and that would take about forty-five minutes." Now that was when all things came together, and timing was everything—the doors of past influencers opened back up.

My parents came to the farm for the day to visit (initial influencers). So, as we went back downtown and turned at the main stop light, I could see my cousin, Frankie, sitting in his jeep at his real estate office. We stopped to visit Frankie. It had been a good while since I saw him. He invited us in for some coffee. We visited and looked at old family pictures of my great-grandparents and of their fiftieth anniversary. With my parents being there, I thought it was cool that all these years later, the grandchildren and great-grandchildren were looking at their ancestors when they were kids. Frankie has been a life-time influencer on me. He spent years overseas with Brown and Root Caught behind enemy lines when the first Gulf War broke out, he and two others came up with a plan to get back across to safety. He was mentioned in the Wall Street Journal. He is seventy-seven and still setting goals and working on them. At this stage of the game, only the goals matter. He says, "One more real estate sale, and I'll make my goal for the year."

I left for a few minutes to pick up the shredder before returning to the real estate office. As we left, I told my mom, "Let's eat across the street before we head back."

So, as I walked in, I saw my other cousin and her husband—her dad, an influencer of mine, is President and owner of Circle Y Saddle Company International. As we went over to greet them, I saw my Uncle 's (who passed too early) brother, who I have not seen since the funeral (nine years from then). Soon, folks from Edna walked in. I have not seen them in about the same time. I sat back and thought, "How does that happen? Having this many connections to my past influencers within thirty yards all in the same day." So, it hit me—don't lose the opportunity. After we all ate and were walking out, I leaned down to talk to the now eighty-five-year-old brother, who is sharp as a tack, and as we shook hands he held on tight while we looked each other in the eyes and talked about my uncle and how much we missed him. What was funny is what he told me—it was as if my uncle were there—he went right into something only a few folks know. I knew what he was saying, what it was about, and why he said it (it needed no background or reasoning, just something that needed to be made straight). He told me how my uncle would have handled it. That was an important talk, and I'm so glad it happened and I got to see him. Then, I did not let the last one pass me by either as one of my parents' friends from Edna asked about Melyn. I knelt down and told her how much her husband influenced me and what a huge impact he had on me as a mentor. I don 't think she ever knew and was elated and was going to tell him.

So, as I wrapped up the day, I wondered how that many life influencers all ended up in the same place and in the same time period—all coming in from different directions, with different reasons for being there, and none knowing the other's plans. Some days are just pretty cool!

I think we should never underestimate the power of influence we have over others. We do and, to what extent, we may never know. Some days it may be small, just a smile to lighten up their day and then other days it may be bigger as we make their dreams a reality. A dream to own a home, grow a company, or get that car they always wanted. These are ways we help others with the needs they have at hand. But always know it is more than the deal or transaction—it is how they feel when they walk out the doors, and what lasting influence it made in their life. Just like all those folks that walked back into my life this past Saturday (from when I am writing this). I am so thankful for each of them and what they did for me, how each treated me and the examples of how they made their lives into what they are today.

Lasting and most crucial—life changing.

"Show yourself in all respects to be a model of good works,

and in your teaching show integrity, dignity."

—Titus 2:7

2

"What is the most important part of your day?"

EVERY DAY STARTS with me reviewing and updating my legal pad with my list of things to accomplish. That list gets updated sometimes several times a day, and it's the first thing in the morning that gets prioritized. This Friday was no different. Fridays for the most part are the busiest as they are full of weekly wrap-ups—it's the last day of the week. This Friday on my list was the opportunity to speak outside the bank.

I received the invitation to speak a few weeks back, and I was honored to have the opportunity for the Bank and me to do so. The invite was from a high school consumer finance class. So, as the class time came close, Kim asked me what I was going to speak on and after my initial thought was revealed on what I thought was going to be witty and acceptable was quickly "not accepted". By the way, do you think someone who has taught school for over twenty-two years would know more than me? The last time I spoke to a class was with one of Kim's Junior High classes back in Gonzales, where the subject matter quickly moved from banking to "Did you really grow up with Stone Cold Steve Austin?" So, my time in the class room was full of stories of us growing up together. And yes, the planned banking talk was quickly kicked off to the side.

So, as the day started, Charley came into my office and we planned the talk and how that was going to all lay out. She suggested we both talk about the journey into overall banking as well as specific banking products. I thought that was an excellent idea. That's what inspired this "thought for the week." My mind raced back to fifth grade when the local banker came to speak to my class, which gave me the spark for banking. So, I thought of how we could influence and hopefully put interest into one or a few of those kids and speak life and encouragement to all. That really made me want to do a good job and connect with the students. My thought was, "This is the most important thing I will do today." I wanted to do my best to reach those that needed to hear what I would say. It was about that banker who took the time to come to my class forty-one years ago to make me think about my future. Maybe just maybe, I could return the favor and do the same.

"For the length of days and years of life a
nd peace they will add to you.
—Proverbs 3:2

3

"Thank folks before it's too late."

THE THOUGHT STARTED last Sunday with me thinking about lunch after Mass. Thinking of a hamburger, and my mind for whatever reason went to my grandparents and the trip when they took me to Six Flags when I was in early grade school. Every meal was at the Pit Grill, and I chose a hamburger and nothing else. When I took the job at the Dallas FED, one of the first meals Kim and I had was at the Pit Grill to relive a memory. When we drove up all those years later on North Collins Street—there it was—still the same. It ended up being not far from our apartment as we settled into Arlington. By the way, I just ran google on it and I'm sorry to see it has since closed.

Meals have always been a time for me to be thankful. We talked about the day at lunch with Melyn in College Station. Kim told Melyn, "I could put a bowl of cereal in front of your dad for dinner and he would never complain." I think that is in part to an impression my grandparents had on me. Being with both sets of them a lot growing up, allowed me to see the impact of the depression and how hard they would work to raise some of their staples. There were no doubts about the thanks that was offered at every table gathering. I think the other reason is, since I don 't cook (properly), having a good meal prepared by my mom everyday growing up after she worked all day was always a blessing. The same goes with Kim now. I don 't take that for granted. I realize the efforts taken to prepare a dinner and the clean-up afterwards.

Then I remember very well, starting off on our own, when a hamburger was a very big deal and the fries and drink were not an option. Not forgetting the past is always so real when I sit down. It's that little thing (in real life thing), for whatever reason, that brings reality to me—whether it be a fine dinner out, at home, or just a quick opening of a can of something. It has never left my mind to be thankful.

Being a grateful initiator makes for such an attitude lifter. It's better than the alternative—looking for something not just right. It affects your thoughts and reality.

I always wonder, "Did I say thank you enough to my grandparents, so they knew the memories they created for me and the sacrifices were appreciated? I knew it took a sacrifice for them to take off from work and spend hard-earned money to make that trip.

Saying *"Thank You"* is probably the most powerful phrase one can say to another. It shows respect for the other's efforts, thoughtfulness, hard work, and sacrifices. It shows we acknowledge the benefits that we gain individually and cooperatively from their actions. The key wording is: we benefit. That value or betterment we in some aspect gain from someone else. Because of that, the least we can say are those little words. The funny part is for someone to do all the work in exchange for another to say, *"Thank You"* seems like a pretty good deal for the receiver.

Let's never forget folks have a choice when banking with financial services. We should always use our number one value of respect and always show appreciation and gratitude in all we do. Folks work very hard to get what they have to survive in this world. Everyone deserves that sign of "thanks" immediately, not later or maybe when. We should never have an opportunity where we say, "Should have thanked them! Now it's too late."

This week made me think about all the things folks have done for me. I sure hope I paid my respects back and did it enough so they really knew and had no doubts. I am sure I did not do a good enough job along the way and missed some. I was very thankful before a few folks passed that I ensured my heartfelt gratitude, and in one case not knowing it would be the last time I saw them. Thankful for that last time and last opportunity to tell him you made an impact on me and "I appreciate you."

A good rule to end all transactions and conversations with a truly meant and heartfelt *"Thank You"*.

"In everything give thanks..."
—1 Thess. 5:18

4

"Seeing the accomplishments of others can make you appreciate things more."

I FINALLY SAW something this weekend that I was not able to truly grasp until now. Melyn got her reward for seventeen years of education on Friday. She made it, and Kim and I are so proud of her—second generation to now have graduated from a University.

As I looked forward to her graduating from school, my mind was on her next steps in life and her near move to California. But the last two weeks have also caused me to slow down a bit and take it all in, not move so fast, and think about right now. Knowing right now is what we have all worked so hard for and Kim and I prepared for this day and her journey. All that time saving money to get her through school and all of Kim's efforts from kindergarten to today on her education highway. I can honestly say a huge thank you to Kim for it was all her that took care of every academic oversight, need, and prodding along the way. So, I am thankful that I sat back just a bit and put it in neutral and just watched and took it all in.

The day arrived and reality was here. There we were in the stands with the family and Melyn was somewhere in the hallway waiting to come in. Yes, I was thinking about the Methodist preschool, Happy House, Gonzales grammar school and Junior High, King Ranch Jr. High School, and Riviera High School graduations for sure. This was the big one—the last one at this point in her life. Then the music kicked in and they all walked, and it finally started to hit me what it was all about for Melyn and the uniqueness of Texas A&M University. That was something I had not truly grasped until that moment. I watched her walk the stage and I was filled with pride as she did it, taking the diploma. My little girl is now a Major University Grad. It was a lengthy graduation, and I stepped out to take a call before returning right before the final commencement closing. That was when I felt it—as the music started up and the cheers started. I knew then what it was all about as my flesh and blood was now part of the Former Student Association.

Life is really cool as "you never say never" and you "never really know how things will turn out," This was a great journey and for me to take the time to sit back and see what was going on. To live it just a bit through Melyn, showed me the appreciation of something that I never really understood before that day.

We should always appreciate others' efforts. Folks work hard for what they acquire in life. Some things like the above in education can be easy to pass by when you see the paper on the wall. But, we have to stop and think how hard it was to get it. To think about all the work, time and sacrifice that it took to get that single piece of paper. Other things may be more tangible but all take someone working their tails off to obtain, to reach their goals, and to earn a living.

We should always be cognizant of others' efforts as those need to be recognized and appreciated. This week, when you see someone who did a good job, maybe they made a personal goal or worked very hard to gain something they value in life, recognize that and praise them on their accomplishment and let them know that was an accomplishment and they should be proud of that.

Life is not always easy and to get to where you want to be takes very hard work and sacrifices.

Let's be encouragers to all those around us, and I guarantee you it will flow back on us.

"Therefore encourage one another just as you are doing."

—1 Thess. 5:11

5

"Surprise someone with something they would have never suspected, and see what happens next."

I THINK EVERYONE enjoys a nice surprise, something they did not expect or it exceeded their expectations. Actually the definition of a surprise is:

1. To encounter suddenly or unexpectedly; take or catch unawares.
2. To attack or capture suddenly and without warning.
3. To cause to feel wonder, astonishment, or amazement, as at something unanticipated *(This is the surprise we want)*.
4. To cause (someone) to do or say something unintended.
5. To elicit or detect through surprise.

So, what surprises you? If this is Christmas time, this is the season that gifts will be given; what will you give and what will you receive? Will it be more than the monetary aspect alone?

I was given a gift this weekend that I would have never expected, and it will be one of my favorite gifts, one that I will have with me daily. For years I have wanted this gift. One of my former bank directors was a rancher, and he had two of them. Every time I would go ride horses or work cattle on his ranch, they were there. Melyn grew up with one of them, and the last time we were in Gonzales we had to stop by the ranch to see it. Others have them around, and I always thought it would be cool to have one. I had been asking for one for years, and it just never happened. So, this year I asked for one knowing it would probably not happen.

Late Saturday afternoon, Kim, Melyn, and I were getting ready to have dinner and an early Christmas with some friends. As we were waiting to leave, I made the comment, "How is what I asked for going to fit in one of those boxes under the tree?" Kim's response was, "It's not there." Kidding, of course, as I knew it was not going to happen, I made a few more comments. As we drove over for dinner, I made the comment, "I don 't think it's good to leave that gift in the wrapped box for the next two days." Again, Kim said, "You're not getting that." My response was, "If you're going to disappoint me, wait till Christmas morning to do it, and let me have two more days to think about the possibility of getting the gift I was hoping for." Again, kidding of course. When we got to the guest's home, I was telling them about my comments, and we were kidding around about what I really wanted. We had a great dinner, and then it was time to open presents. The young kids opened theirs first and then the older ones started. So, Melyn's boyfriend handed Kim a gift, which I did not see her open, but it was tied to mine. A few got it quickly and started to laugh. Then I heard him tell his sister, "Go get Mr. Stary's gift." I saw her hand him an Easter-type basket. I was wondering what it was as I was really not expecting a gift to begin with. He grabbed it as she walked into the room, and then handed me the basket. When he reached out to give it to me, I could see what was in the basket. It was what I had wanted for years—I'd been talking about that night. He had given me that gift—unexpectedly. He knew it was what I was wanting, and he bought it for me as a special gift. Some of you may have guessed by this time what was in the basket. It was an Australian

Blue Heeler "cow dog" puppy. I was totally surprised and taken aback.

This showed me a lot about this young man. It showed me he was willing to take the time to find something special that I really wanted and he knew me well enough to know that. He spent his own money to get it, and I know this young man worked very hard to earn that money. By the way, that young man is now my son-in-law, Jacob. So that meant a lot that he sacrificed for me. The dog will be very special to me, but even more for who gave it to me and how that came about. That makes the gift even more valuable and meaningful. I will have this dog close to me because loyalty is one of the main character traits of this breed.

There are good surprises and not so good surprises. We want to prevent and avoid the bad ones; we don't want any "now that was a surprise" in a shocking or disappointing way. To avoid those types of surprises, we must over-communicate (written and verbal), be 110 percent accurate, practice excellence in all we do, be on time or faster, over-deliver, and allow no room for any surprise to raise its head. Now, what should we be doing in delivering good surprises as I was given in the above story? Give surprises in a way that you would when you give "gifts" to someone you think highly of or respect. Service and product "surprises" should be like an unexpected gift. Things that would cause the receiver to think, "ow! I did not expect that! That was much much better than my expectations." Things that would make them feel great and blown away. Their reactions should be, "I can't believe that was that easy," "That was a great product or service experience," "They turned my request much quicker than I could imagine," "I am sticking here and nowhere else," "Everyone is going to hear about this," "It was just like they told me and even better," and "They were true professionals all the way—there were no hidden surprises". Bottom line is, we need to focus and think what we do everyday is like giving gifts. Just like any really good gift, it requires a sacrifice on us. Those sacrifices come in our time, efforts, making sure everything is just right, knowing what the customer really wants and needs, knowing what is important to them, knowing where the value lies and what it is going to take to deliver beyond their expectations. We never want to give a gift that the receiver is asking for a refund or exchange on.

Let's give surprise "gifts" everyday to all we serve.

"But earnestly desire the greater gifts..."

—1 Cor. 12:31

6

"Perceptions are like rocks, and we need not leave them lying around."

AS THE OLD saying goes, *perceptions are reality.* Whether we like this fact or not—true, half true, and maybe all together false—perceptions matter, and they affect how others see things and how things may eventually turn out. Perceptions can change final outcomes or directions. If you consider that perceptions are real, and what others see in a person, or perceive to be the case, is true, what do you do? They are a real driver in some cases. Thus my thought for the week: "Perceptions are like rocks, and we can't leave them lying around." Rocks are those things you can change, control, or influence that are lying around for others to pick up and throw.

Here are a few points I found to consider when researching "perceptions are realities":

1. **"You may or may not have control over the events in your life, but you can certainly take control of how to respond to them.** That part of life will always be within your power. This is where life gets interesting because you shape your own reality through your beliefs.
2. **There is no such thing as reality.** There is only "your" version of it which is essentially your perception. Remember that what you believe to be true is only as true as your worldly experience and it doesn't go any further than that. Many scientific theories are just that, theories! It doesn't make them true.
3. **It's important to note that how you choose to perceive things is how they come across to you.** I believe that your power to choose how to perceive things makes them appear that way to you.
4. **Everything begins with a decision—decide now to be in charge of your own perception of reality.** Because if you don't, there are plenty of folks whose sole purpose in life is to craft that perception for you.

5. **We can all agree that perception is reality.** Based on our experiences in the physical world, the many opinions people hold and the different ways of viewing and describing the VERY SAME things, it's only rational, logical, and feasible to conclude that perception is in fact reality.

The above focuses on our decision to decide how to react. In other words, how to fix it.

My point is we all have areas that others perceive about us. These perceptions can be about our personality traits, work skills, abilities, and character traits. Let me say again, **what one initially thinks of another** is the important thing I want to drive home. These perceptions can be both strengths and weaknesses. Let's focus on the weaknesses for this week's thought. The question is to all, what do others perceive in me? What are those perception "rocks" that we all need to work on and pick up? What are those rocks that we all need to go pick up before they get thrown back at us? In this example, when using the rock-throwing analogy, I am referring to all those things that you can control and take away from the perception issue. For example, someone may have a perception issue of someone being a bad driver. If that person has had a few wrecks, is getting speeding tickets, insurance cancellations, and scares people when they are driving, guess what, they probably are a bad driver and they need to slow down and quit getting tickets (pick up the rocks). On the other hand, if they are not then they have to stop that perception and figure out why that perception is there and prove to those that think that (pick up the rocks) by taking them on a ride and correcting their perceptions. Prove otherwise and **show** your record and **performance.**

To me, it means getting back to being fully accountable for ourselves and our actions. Taking the rocks away is being proactive, being ahead of others, protecting reputations, and building a true picture not a perceived one. To me it puts all in a better position if we become fully accountable for ourselves first and then we can take away those rocks from others. Then this makes all those with perceptions of us fully accountable themselves with no rocks to pick up. If we can all do this, which means all are accountable, all doing the right things, in an excellent manner then we should all be able to rock and roll.

What we do to a large extent is all about reputation and perceptions. It is based on character, confidence, strength, professionalism, competency, excellent service, delivery, and to be known as the go-to folks. So, do we have the right perceptions and reputations and is every one of those 100 percent on check. If not, if there is only 99 percent, we have a lot of work to do to fix that 1 percent. We all have a daily responsibility to do our very best—both real and perceived. This takes hard work, constant diligence, and the right attitude to address and correct when you need to do so effectively and in an expedient manner. Be 100 percent accountable for yourself 100 percent of the time.

Pick up the rocks and leave none behind.

"...having a reputation for good works..."

—1 Tim. 5:10

7

"There are some jobs that were just meant for two or more people."

I AM ONE that does not like to ask for help in most cases, and I grew up like that. Along the way that has put me in a few tight spots and cost a few dollars, redoes, and touch-up repairs. A lot of one-on-one incidents have occurred but some of them turned out better with no detriments other than a bruise, scraped knuckles, or a sore back, like the time in high school when I got my fingers caught in the fender well underneath my hot rod while it was on jacks. I thought for a minute I would be there a while. Or like other times when I would take the full hardtop off our old model jeep by myself, when the neighbors were outside right across the street. Or the time I took the front-end loader off my tractor, loaded it in the back of my truck and then replaced all by myself. Sometimes it just took a little muscle to get it done and other times it really made me think of what I had at my disposal to make this deal work by myself.

The tractor was a good example of all the extra work I did to use come-along, fifty-five-gallon drums, chains, and slow movements to get that loader, frame, bucket, hydraulics and line all back on and up again. Lining up the bolts on the swing arms when part of the overall unit was suspended by a chain with no wiggle room was no easy task by myself. Got it done!

These times have made me think often that an extra pair of hands would have been nice, like this past weekend when a gate needed an adjustment. The gate had been dragging and really it was an aggravation as every time you would walk it back, it would catch on the ground about half way around. So, when you have a fourteen-foot gate and your reach is only twenty-nine inches, you can't hold the weight of the gate straight out while you adjust the brackets. Then you have to wonder, "How do I hold up the gate higher than it is?" All this time you're knowing that as soon as you loosen the brackets it is going to drop even further and do so quickly. The best I could do was chain up the swinging end much higher on the "catch" post. I did that and, when the brackets loosened, the weight of the gate would push the loosened brackets over and put them out of whack. So, what do you do? You use your reach to hold the gate as far in the middle as you can and then stretch your legs out to cover as much gate as you can. The reach part was to take as much weight off the swinging end so it would not push the loosened brackets out of alignment. Then I would extend my leg as far as I could to then tap the bracket over with the toe of my boot to line it back up. Once I did that, it finally stayed while I carefully held the gate in a line as I moved back over to lean down and tighten the bolt. Definitely a two man job, but hey why ask for help?

I am thinking of going back soon and having Kim with me to film so I can put it on Youtube as "The proper way to align a gate by yourself". I think this could be a retirement check.

I use the above examples of how it would sometimes be better, safer, cheaper, and faster to have someone else help in a few circumstances. Also, collaboration itself can bring about efficiencies and a better end result. I say that after spending a few hours with Greg this Sunday afternoon as a few projects needed to get knocked out. It was much easier to do that with no interruptions and both of us collaborating. We did a day's work as we have time to focus and finish several items we needed done early that week. All were, I think, a much better product than we could have done had we been rushed or interrupted. The content, fullness, and accuracy all due to taking the time to think through what we needed in the end and having two folks crank out the projects worked very well. As each of us added, complemented, and did our own parts.

So, to us this week, what we do is so codependent on each other. Everything we touch is handled and processed by several others in the bank. Knowing that each of us affects the final outcome and no one is by themselves in work, processes, end results or service points, really makes you think this is a job that is for two or more—in our cases many more than that.

Know that and always ask when you need to ensure all is correct, when you need to get a deadline met, time is of the essence. Or, if you think it is important to bring in a coworker on a service point, use the story above as a good example.

We are all in this together and we are successful when we are all working together.

"Two are better than one because they have a good return for their labor. For if either of them falls, the one will lift up his companion. But woe to the one who falls when there is not another to lift him up ... And if one can overpower him who is alone, two can resist him. A cord of three strands is not quickly torn apart."

—Ecc. 4:9-12

8

"Follow-ups are important even well after the point of impact."

THIS PAST WEEK, I saw a call coming in on caller ID from a prior customer. It was someone who sells farm equipment and one I had bought two tractors from. After I moved to Kingsville, I called him on a tractor trade, and we agreed pretty much over the phone. It should have been a smooth easy transition but several things came into play that delayed it. His tractor did not have a front-end loader and I needed that, so he began to call his vendors for one that would fit his tractor. That was the first issue as there was a shortage of hydraulic pumps and only a few companies that make these parts. This went on for a while, calling back and forth, waiting. He told me at one point that my wife must be happy with me and I asked why, and he said, "Because I've never seen a sales deal like this where the other side was so patient." By the way, my wife would disagree and I have never heard that before in my life. I doubt I will ever receive that compliment again in the future.

The front-end loader finally came in and the sales rep brought it from the factory to install. When it was all done, I got a call and made a run to Gonzales to trade tractors. I brought the tractor back and started to use it. One day, while rolling across the pasture, I noticed the front-end loader bucket was not even. I looked down and saw the hydraulic hose was almost pinched in the lift arms. I stopped, got off, and noticed the support brackets had broken. The weld did not hold and the entire loader was inoperable. Which meant I had to take it off in a way that would not further damage the frame or lift parts. I called back to Gonzales and a call was placed to the owner of the loader company. They had found two issues. One, the design needed improvement. Two, more importantly, the welder was doing substandard welds that would break (he was not there long after they found that issue). So, to make a long story short, I managed to take off, disassemble, and ship the loader back to the factory by myself. After I got the loader back, the owner of the company walked me through, over a cell call, the finer details of reassembly (as I had to take off parts that do not normally come off due to the twisting of the A-frame on the disassembly). It was a pain to say the least, to leverage and balance a solid steel A-frame with the loader arms, hydraulic pump shafts and lining all up so that the pivot slots (one side of the tractor then the opposite side of the tractor) can allow the installation of solid pins that have absolutely zero tolerance. All with only a come-along, chain, and small sledge hammer. To say the least, I stepped aside from being a Baptist and reverted back to being a Catholic as I was speaking "French" while doing all of this. Last week's call from the tractor dealer was just to check back to make sure all was still ok.

And that call also opened up a request to "look out" for something else I need.

I thought about this call and appreciated him calling after all that time had passed to check back to make sure all was still working. My point this week is that issues will come up and communication is paramount to getting through it with a **done today right - "DTR" standard.** During the wait on the hydraulic pump, I would get calls each week telling me the status. When I called him about the break, he called the vendor and stayed on it until it was fixed. He never got impatient and simply sorted it out. Here it was a good while later and he just wanted to call to make sure all was still good. He could have just passed on it as there was no longer any responsibility to check back. Those follow-up calls make all the difference, those calls that show caring and the taking of responsibility way after the fact. Those follow-up calls may also lead to other requests as this call did last week. That is the other point; there is a lot of competition out there, but I still believe if we take care of customers and we do all their heavy lifting and make it easy. This is where we add value. In the case above, I did not 1want to shop or trade all over for a tractor or deal with those I didn't know. I knew this man and built a relationship with him and had a trust factor. That **trust factor** came to pass when the break came.

We need to make others' lives easier and take the worry, shop factor, and extra work out of their

lives. Customers have enough to do, worry about, as life is busy and there will always be issues that arise. We have to make their dealings with us pleasurable, in other words, let us do all the work and carry the load and fix issues quickly and correctly when they do occur. Simply put to practice **excellence** in all we do.

Make each customer experience one that exceeds expectations and call back and follow up even way after the point of impact. It makes a difference and keeps the relationships going.

"And I will show you a still more excellent way."
—1 Cor. 12:23

9

"Did you ever watch in anticipation for how big the ice cream scoop was going to be?"

I WILL NEVER forget going to Dairy Queen (DQ) as a kid and getting an ice cream cone through the drive-through. As I watched the lady fill the soft serve ice cream in the cone, I noticed it was getting to be a good size and I was happy. Then I watched her set the ice cream on a small scale to weigh it. I was not sure why she did that until I saw her scoop the ice cream into the trash can as it must have been too big. To this day, I still cannot figure out how giving someone a little bit too much is cheaper than completely throwing out the product or giving another serving. Years later, I hired a DQ manager to work in my former bank and you can imagine what I asked her. She told me they do that to give standard sizes. Again, I do not see how putting too much ice cream on a cone and throwing the whole thing away just to give more makes money?

But think about this. Have you ever watched your server scoop your ice cream? Did you sit in anticipation wondering just how hard they pressed on the ice cream in the big cardboard carton to make a larger ball? Or would they just drag the scoop across the top with little effort and stop there? What about the next guest in line? What did their scoop look like? Now the difference in the soft service at DQ and the ice cream at a creamery, such as Marble Slab, is quality and cost.

But either way, I would bet most folks when it comes to ice cream, whether it is DQ or Marble Slab, would not mind if they got more than the "weight scale" allowed. I think we can all be guilty of that one. The thought we all have is: "Did I get what I thought I was paying for?" When food comes to you in a larger portion, what do you think?

A few years back, Kim and I were invited to have a very nice Christmas outing in Austin, which included a high-end restaurant and musical performance at the theater. The meal was very expensive, but came with only a very very small portion of food right in the middle of the plate. If the china and place settings could have been taken home we might have gotten about a quarter of our money's worth back. The food was very high quality but had absolutely no quantity.

DQ large portions—marble slab small? Quality vs. quantity—what if you had both?

Think what if you could have both!

Just last week, I had to get several loads of dirt to level out our new yard. I was told there were nineteen yards of dirt in each load. How could I know if I got more or less? I will never know. I just have to believe I paid for what I got. Although, I will say that Kim cut the check for less money than the bid was for. So, I think I'm good, and we got what we paid for.

How do you know what size you pay for and what you got? Do we really ever know what we get is what we paid for? Sometimes, if we know the product or service well enough, we do, but what if we are dealing with a product or service that we do not? What if there is no way to check what you bought, like my buying dirt or in the first example ice cream? Both cost money, but the latter was a chunk more money.

What about the folks we touch? Do we give them the larger scoop (service and the right product) of ice cream? If two are in line with one watching, do we give more to one knowing the other customer is watching only to short them a bit? We need to give the customer a scoop (service) bigger than they expect. I think there was an ice cream parlor here in Kingsville a while back called "The Big Scoop". What if folks thought of us as a big scoop of banking? I think we would have a line out the door. Folks, us included, want a deal, and excellent service is paramount in making the "Big Scoop" value. You might say you add toppings or sprinkles (excellent service) on top at no cost.

Press hard and put in some effort when scooping ice cream for our customers. They will come back and tell others if you do.

" ...so that you may approve the things that are excellent, in order to be sincere."

—Phil. 1:10

10

"Do you have a test this week?"

TWO WEEKS AGO at Sunday lunch, I asked this question to Melyn and a friend. I had a couple of reasons to ask this, but one was to make sure there was not a test on Monday that required time to be set aside that afternoon to prepare. If not, then the rest of Sunday was relatively free. After a few comments, Melyn's friend smiled and asked me if I had a test this week. Thus here lies the thought for the week: life itself is a test.

How would you answer the question? I hope all would say 100 percent yes. I said yes, and spoke in generalities of some of the things I would be tested on later in the week. It hit me that we all need to be ready for the daily tests that we face. In banking, we have all sorts of tests: audits, bank exams, loan reviews, second reviews on processes, loan and account approvals, accounts to balance, budgets and goals to meet and these are only some of the many daily tests we must pass each day. We have numerous checks and balances that we deal with daily, just think about our tellers as an example and their daily balancing. If they do their jobs correctly and have no outages, then they get a 100 percent passing grade, if not, someone needs to find and then correct the less than perfect score. Every other account and every transaction in our bank has to balance to an offsetting account. Again, a passing score of 100 percent is required. We must also know that a less than passing grade effects a lot of others in the bank as it sometimes takes several folks to address and fix an error.

Then there is the entire service test we must pass as well. The goal of providing excellent service and exceeding customer expectations. That includes both internal and external customers. Getting a perfect score on every customer contact is a tough test to meet, but one we must strive for daily. Think back over last week, if you were graded on every customer service point and touch how would you grade yourselves? Now how would the customer grade you? How would an objective third party grade you? If any of these three were not 100 perfect how would you correct those interactions? How are you going to improve? More importantly, do you strive to live up to the grade of every test? I hope we are all reaching for that perfect score as our coworkers and customers both desire that attention, passion, and internal drive from us.

Third, think about the test of carrying our own weight and contributing to the bottom line? All of us and everything we do affects the bottom line, in our service points, our operations humming along at full capacity, our every transaction balancing and accurate, and each of us generating income and lessening the expense side. We all have a part no matter what we do in affecting the bottom line. Every one of us should take on the understanding that "what I do personally is imperative to the bank, and I can change the outcome of everything I touch, do, or say—I am a game changer." Every one of us doing excellence is imperative to our overall success.

Lastly, the most important test may be the one we don't see, those tests that others give us that will show our very core and our skill level without us being 100 percent ready or even aware. This test may be the eyes that are always watching us. Passing these tests is important because they show our true colors and they either take away or add doubt, they will show our true intentions, they will build or take away trust and confidence.

Perception is reality and that is why every contact we have sets the tone and mindset of others. We may only have one test to pass or fail from another person. You just never really know how others may be testing, but they are and they want to see your reaction, your skill set and knowledge, your character, your body language, and your intentions just to state a few things. What lasting image will we leave them with? It may be something so small you may never even realize it and at other times it may be very obvious. Either way a grade will come thereafter and a low grade may be hard to overcome later. That is why we should always be on guard, keep our perceptions high, and watch our Ps and Qs, our speech (accuracy and clarity) as well as all our actions or reactions (what we do and what we deliver on) in the highest professional and respectful regard .

If we do our jobs to our utmost, be a true professional, practice excellence, always know someone is watching and practice the bank's core values, we will be on track to get that passing grade.

"Test my mind and my heart..."

—Ps. 26:2

11

"What would your current life mission statement be, and do others see you deliver that commitment daily?"

THE LAST SEVERAL weeks, I worked with a select committee to facilitate a new mission statement for a foundation that I serve on. The current mission statement was revised by a board member who saw a need for a refocus, to separate us from other foundations and provide a clearer vision. This revised mission will give the foundation a distinction that will give no doubts of who we are, what we stand for, and our purpose that differentiates us from all others. The mission statement has five strong character points that are incorporated in the new focus. All traits have been proven and tested by those in the past, current, and the future of that group we are entrusted to promote.

As I read the new mission statement, it made clear to me that this statement, worthy of being written on paper by one and agreed to by others, has true meaning. It has been well thought out and supported by many things that all tie back to the written words. It has history, defendable character traits, action, and foresight. A mission statement is in writing and agreed to by those that are entrusted to carry out the agreement (contract). As I was working on a draft pledge-drive letter this weekend for the same foundation, I initiated the letter with the new mission statement. Why? Again, it is a written contract of purpose and what the purpose of commitment is for today and for others to follow in the future. It is a plan of action—better yet, a MAP. If someone is going to commit to something, they need to clarify what the plan is, where we are headed and what is my part and future. All have to commit, everyone, to ensure the mission is carried out.

So, I am sure you have read a mission statement from other organizations. What do you think when you read them? Have there been any that you read and say, "WOW that is deep and meaningful"? Could you buy into that vision and run? Have you read others that you think, "What were these folks drinking? This makes no sense. It has no provision for today, much less the future." If you wrote a mission statement for yourself what would it say? Would it incorporate character traits, ethics, hard work, and other values? Would it be for the betterment of others and their future as well? Would it be clear and future-oriented? As noted above, would it be a map for others to treasure one day?

We are unique in that we have a founder who started our bank with a vision and we use his quote today: "T**o help those who showed the spirit of cooperation in community building."** A few key words: **helping others**—*using the bank's resources to help others accomplish their goals and make their visions a reality;* **who showed the spirit of cooperation**—*working with those who know they are needed to make things happen and want to do their part;* and **community building**—*a vision to build a community for those yet to come.* Think about those words written over 100 years ago. They live on and are still in practice today. Reading those words, do you first, agree? Second, do you get the deeper meaning? Third, will you be committed and live those principles out daily as one of the select few that are part of Kleberg Bank, entrusted to carry this on?

A mission statement that is wholly of sacrifice is entrusted to the current generation to pass on to the future generation.

"Where there is no vision the people perish."

—Proverbs 29:18

12

"If you had a rewind button, how many times per week would you use it?"

THINK BACK TO last week. If you had a rewind button, would you use it? If not then congratulations, you had a perfect week. Now for the other 99.99999 percent of you, would you have to use it a lot or maybe just once. Now think, would you use it over for something you should have learned from a prior experience and this is a repeat? This point is very important as everyone can have a second sight on things, but not learning from it is not what a "wishful rewind" would work for.

I think I can safely say, if there were such a thing as a rewind button, it would probably be the most used invention in the world, and the inventor would be worth zillions of dollars.

As I have said before, there is more than enough gray in life for us to add to it. Having a rewind button would be a great tool to fix those, "Man, I should have done that, should have done that a little bit better, should have said that or should not have spoken at all, should have double checked that one more time, or asked that one more question." I think even in a week when all went well there is always something that could have been better, as there is really nothing that is absolutely 110 percent perfect and could not use improvement. We live in an imperfect world but we need to do our very best to practice excellence in all things, make things that we have control of or input in better and never add to the norm, be average, or make things worse.

So, what do we do when the rewind button is not there? I think there are several things.

1. Be real and see what really happened, learn from it, and don't allow that to happen again.
2. Take a breath, step back, and see what needs to be done to correct and quickly prioritize those options.
3. Act, this is the mature action as sometimes this is where you can make things a bit worse or really bad.

Consider the future at this point and see what needs to be done as you look forward for the betterment of all, remember who you represent—this is beyond just you personally. Keep the personalities to a minimum or out altogether. Most things we deal with are today and right now, but there are those things that are much bigger and will take more thinking as they will have future ramifications. Having said that, do not allow procrastination or double-think to get in the way of trying to fix or rectify something. Time lost not addressing an issue is an enemy.

Not all things that at first glance seem permanent are not fixable errors or mistakes. In other words, if there are correct actions taken with timely wisdom (a well thought out plan of corrective action) and you have the right attitude there are options and it can be fixed, then in most cases the outcome, although not what was originally expected, may turn out better. It has been said that all things happen for a reason. As I get older, I have found this to be very true, but only if you look hard at the why, react with much consideration and review all the options there after. It is up to us alone to adjust, react correctly, and look forward to what is the very best outcome and how can we turn this around for the very best. It works and sometimes the other outcomes will surprise you. I have seen things at times, thinking, "How in the world is this going to be fixable or tum out for the good?" I can say it can and will if you have a true personal will, know we have been entrusted with a great responsibility to be stewards of what we have been given, show the sacrificial diligence, don't quit, ask for help from others and bring in the support, keep doing the right thing, and keep what is important in front at all times.

We don't have a rewind button so we have to do our very best first, listen to that little voice that warns us, take time to think before we act or speak, and when a "rewind" is needed, do everything that is required to remedy the situation or error.

We must always remember we are stewards first.

"In this case, moreover, it is required of stewards that one befound trustworthy."

—1 Cor. 4:2

13

"It is in the eyes of what is being seen and felt."

THERE ARE A lot of ways to say things like: "Beauty is in the eyes of the beholder", "See it through the eyes of someone else", "Walk in another man's shoes", and we can go on from there with others. But after a certain concert this last week, it made me really think about looking at life through other people's eyes and finding what they see.

Frankie Valli and the 4 Seasons (not the first group, but a new generation) performed at the historical Majestic Theater in downtown San Antonio. All the ambiance of those factors together, you just don't get any better than that.

In part of the show, Mr. Valli spoke to and interacted with the audience. He said his first influence with show business was when he was six years old and his mother took him to a Frank Sinatra performance in NYC. He spoke of the life-shaping event like it just happened and how that hooked him into his life today. He went on to speak of his first songs and then on to the rest of his journey during the concert. He would stop between songs at times and tell their backgrounds.

The concert was amazing as the new 4 Seasons did all the dance moves of the past and added a few new ones in perfect union. The harmonies were unbelievable—on spot, on tune, and right on time. Mr. Valli hit every note as though he was still a young man—hammered every song. The song I liked best was the most emotional and moving part of the show. I told someone, now I know why "Goodfellas" have a misty eye during Italian operas. They all came out center stage, the lights went dim. Then they lit up a bit to reveal the four to almost light up like huge shadows. Mr. Valli then walked in between and we heard the beginning of "Silence is Golden." The song went in and out of acapella with a full band several times and the lights were thrown on the images of the four to show them again. Then it was back to Mr. Valli leading the almost mystical performance. The harmony and sound astonished the crowd, while a hush rolled over as all sat and listened to the artists at work.

All the way through the concert, I could not help but wonder what was going on inside Mr. Valli's head.

He is now eighty-two years old He used to stand on the street corner, singing with a group of "Jersey Boys" in the late '50s. Now, all that time later, he is the star of the show—still in charge of the audience, still knocking out the notes, all the lows and highs. Nothing has changed, nothing, except a little outside aging. He is still the same on the inside. I wondered what he thinks when he walks out on stage. Does he still hear the original guys behind him? Does he think of the daughter he lost? Or the other hardships along the way? Does the performance of this day make him think back? Or is it just today's audience and the still-huge future ahead? His eyes have seen a lot, but yet they still see the audience—just a little wear on the outside. Having said that, he still looks and acts like you would think a very mature teen idol who has aged professionally and gracefully would. Maybe his original idol "Old Blue Eyes" helped shape him into what he is today? Pure class. Yes, still today, the women in the crowd rushed the stage and the crowd stood up to move to the front and hold him for three encore songs. He still has it!

Seeing life from another viewpoint can be a huge benefit and serve to assist us as we do our best ever each day in taking care of others. Being sensitive to what they really need and not just what we think they need or hear in part is of the utmost importance. Like that utmost attention that the audience gave to the song, "Silence is Golden." Now think about that, the one song that got the audience's attention to a hush was "Silence is Golden." Sometimes we just have to listen.

The other point to make is the life influences. I bet Frank Sinatra never thought a six-year-old boy in the audience would be so influenced that he would grow up to be an international singing star as well. You never know who is watching and what influence you bring to others or really who they may even turn out to be one day.

Seeing life in a way that is sensitive to hearing the real needs and wants of others goes a long way.

"The hearing ear, and the seeing eye..."
—Proverbs 20:12

14

"Uniqueness cannot be copied."

UNIQUENESS IS DEFINED as "having no like or equal; unparalleled; incomparable—existing as the only one or as the sole example; single; solitary in type or characteristics—limited to a single outcome or result; without alternative possibilities." Or, simply put: "Nothing else like it."

This thought hit me hard as I heard the news of Merle Haggard's passing away this week on his seventy-ninth birthday. I'm not sure why folks passing like that affects me, but the same feeling hit me when George Jones and other strong and gifted artists left us. It makes me think because folks like these are so unique and have made such an influence in their fields that they leave big gaps behind them. Their legacies live on, but their lives cannot be replaced. So that was on my mind on Friday while driving to College Station when "Mama's Hungry Eyes" played and I listened more carefully and appreciated more of his clear and unambiguous uniqueness that will not be copied. Then, right after that, Tammy Wynette and Glen Campbell hit the radio. I thought, "Man, there are three unique voices that all impacted country music and a lot of folks with their song. Two passed and one incapacitated—none ever to preform again, only their taped voices to live on."

So, on the way back home I heard a prior interview with Merle Haggard, it covered how he started, the early influences (and how he carried on those true western-singer pioneers' traditions and foundations always), his mom, the trials, but also the once-in-a-lifetime opportunities, those doors that he walked through just at the right time with the right folks that all lined up to make him the star he was. Listening to him, it was about being honest first and then the music. They talked about his style and what separated him from all the others. And the question, "What is your favorite song?" His response: "Footlights" and its lyrics of "I live the kinda life most men only dream of. I make my livin' writin' songs and singin' them. But I'm forty-one-years old and I ain't got no place to go when it's over. So I hide my age and make the stage and try to kick the footlights out again."

He loved what his talent and opportunities gave to him and allowed him to do. That is to be himself and do it his way. I think another big reason for his success was that he really got the essence of life and turned those into lyrics that grabbed people's heartstrings around the world. I enjoyed hearing his thoughts and reasons for "Momma Tried" and "Mama's Hungry Eyes," and how they were about his mom. "Okie from Muskogee" was in honor of his dad. "Footlights" has lyrics about his dream. "Today I started loving you again" was about an ex-wife. I looked online for the reasons for other songs and they are deep with long lists of rational life lessons..

Merle Haggard is just one of the many who used their God-given talents to make a difference in the world. His talents developed into a persona that emulated his unique personality, style, and outward appearances. All of that pours into the lyrics and songs that will live on way into the future. His uniqueness will never be copied.

Uniqueness cannot be copied. I think the above is an excellent example of individual uniqueness and how that impacts the world. One person using their talents, not in waste but to bring the essence of everyday life into reality for many folks in lyrics and song. We all can do the same everyday by using those given talents to the max. Again, to review the definition of uniqueness "having no like or equal; unparalleled; incomparable—existing as the only one or as the sole example; single; solitary in type or characteristics—limited to a single outcome or result; without alternative possibilities."

For us, think, what if every customer encounter was the same consistent perfection of "limited to a single outcome or result; without alternative possibilities"? Every touch was an excellent, perfect, and caring touch that creates a unique banking experience no one else can replicate.

That, folks, is when we reach the ultimate, and we get to where we need to be. Use your talent wisely and create wonderful outcomes.

"I am fearfully and wonderfully made;
your works are wonderful"
—Ps. 139:14

15

"Never underestimate the power of appreciation."

THIS WEEK, THE above thought was on my mind as I sent you the Friday update. The bottom line of always being thankful and saying that as a salutation in any verbal or written communication shows class and sincerity to the other party.

Late last week, I sent you the quick reminder to always be thankful and show it. I have been seeing some great feedback from our "Thank you for your service" initiative. It is great to see the feedback when a former service person responds with "Thank you for saying that" or "It was my pleasure to serve". That shows not only our appreciation for their time served and personal sacrifice, but also our core value of respect.

To that end, several other thank yous and appreciations were noticed and, I hope, were as impactful as those few that I saw first-hand.

Ending the week on a high note was an encouraging personal email I received that not only made me very thankful but also very humbled. Humbled because the email was from an international artist and motivational speaker and his wife. I hold them in high professional regard because of their extreme talents and gifts. I met him at IBAT years back. It all started with a very cool encounter. Catching a football pass in the middle of an auditorium packed with bankers gave me the opportunity to be on stage with this talent. That encounter left Kim with an original painting of the Statue of Liberty that has hung in her classes in Kingsville and now at TIVY. A constant reminder of how talent and efforts from one individual can reach, touch, or inspire students. The artist and I had a great visit after the IBAT meeting, and he has been on my "thought for the week" list ever since. The personal email will be kept in my notes and hopefully put in my compilation of Thoughts later. But it dazzled me to get this encouragement from a person who travels the world doing motivational speaking and presenting his artwork. This note verified to me what I always hoped my weekly thoughts would bring about.

The artist is sending me a copy of his new book called *The Spark and the Grind* based on "The world is full of dreamers" and "The world needs dreamers who do". I have always said the world is a small place for those who do. I can't wait to get this book and get more of it out to you. I know one thing about the writer is his talent and gift was completely stifled by one person, so much so that he stopped before he even got started. Not until a life-changing event occurred did he draw deep down to that buried talent and passion. That was when his gift rose up. Today he travels all over the world inspiring lives and pulling dreams out of folks. I have thought back on him over the years to our talk that night and how one person's discouragement and personal dream-killer words almost stopped him from reaching huge audiences all over the world. I think we have all had one or more naysayers and discouragers in our lives to whom we can and should say the new coin phrase "Wrong" as Erik did. Thank God he did, as should everyone else as well. No one drives your life, but you! Grab the wheel and take your foot off the brake!

The personal exchange of thanks and appreciation is a powerful tool and should be used often . We have the power to change a person's day with just a few words and our actions. Being appreciative is truly transparent and sincerity can be easily seen. Folks see when you really mean it, when you really want them here and when you are really thankful they are a part of our banking family. There are things in life one can control and being gracious and thankful are two of the things that all can control and impact.

Let's press forward this week with the "Thank you for your service", but keep on with all others we touch in all communications—verbal, written, all tech venues—that we leave no doubts of being gracious, thankful and above all appreciative.

"Brothers, if you have a message of encouragement for the people, please speak."
—Acts 13:15

16

For those who sacrifice – thanks is to be given."

SACRIFICE HAS BEEN on my mind for a couple of weeks and that gets me to the thought this week. There are several words that are linked to sacrifice when you look up the meaning and background of the word. The most meaningful to me and to this thought is "enduring the loss of". Words which relate to this are: "give, devote, pay, dedicate, commit, consecrate—entirely to a specific person, activity, or cause; to free, give up, release, relinquish, resign—part with a possession or right". To me, the bottom line is: **Sacrifice is making a choice to give.** That is to give something of value (time, effort, money, intellect, talents, your vision or thoughts, passion, and maybe even your life) toward something or somebody.

This past week, I was moved by three stories I heard about women who gave their lives for the sake of others. As the verse goes, "There is no greater love than that of a man who gives his life for his friends". All these were in the Sandy Hook Elementary School. One woman hid the children in cabinets and closets, and stood by herself to face the wrath, the second rushed head on, nothing in hand to do what she could, and the third held on to one of the innocent, giving the last bit of comfort and protection. Folks, that is sacrifice to the very end. Nothing in life can top those giving their lives for others. I know people who have had to make these same types of choices and, to me, those are true heroes.

Most of us will never have to make the choice to make the ultimate sacrifice, but we do have the choice everyday to sacrifice in other ways. When I think about daily sacrifices the first person who comes to my mind is my dad. No doubts, the very best example of one who sacrifices for someone else and who always puts others first. I grew up watching my dad work his tail off, spending tons of time at the office, working nights and weekends. He gave that job 110 percent. He also did other things outside his primary job to help out as well. He even worked it out where we could clean the offices and mow the grass. Every week or so, he would get me to sign the back of that check as that money was to be saved for later. He kept books on the side, and he bought a small store to help an elderly man out. When this store was up for sale, Dad bought it and let Jack keep on running it like he had for most of his life. By the way, Jack's picture is one of those on my home desk that I see and think back on often. Dad would run by to check on Jack during the week and keep the books. I would help stock shelves after school and on the weekends when needed. That is where I learned a lesson that I still have not forgotten about counting change backwards. The first time working there by myself one night, I gave a man back about $10 too much. He knew as he looked at me, even when he put it in his pocket.

My dad partnered on cattle and a pair of rental houses. He was always hustling "making payroll" for the family. He would always find a way to make things work, and he did it the right way. My dad showed me how important it was to work hard and provide for a family. I cannot ever remember my dad buying something for himself. I knew there were plenty of things he would have wanted, but he would not do it and even after all these years he will still not do things for himself. It was always his family first, and I saw him, many times, give and do things for others outside our family as well. He never gave those times and. sacrifices a second thought.

I grew up hunting, and as soon as I could handle a rifle, Dad let me shoot from then on—it was not about him. He saved the hunting for me and the time was for us together. This work ethic and sacrificing for the family was instilled into Dad by his father and grandfathers, and those traits are very easy to see among my family. I am thankful to have had those times when I worked with Dad at the store, with the cattle, and even, very early on, mowing and cleaning the office. Those early times taught me the value of work and to be responsible. Dad, thanks for all the sacrifices.

We make choices everyday and those choices, no matter how big or small, will require something from us (sacrifice) to be real, meaningful, and life changing. Those choices will require mentioned previously: commit, devote, and give. Those words are words of doing—they are words of action—they are words of passion and words that require things to be done in an excellent manner, which alone will take a focused commitment (sacrifice). What we do and how we do it every day is really that important. When we choose to interact, we can and do affect and change outcomes in others. Even the smallest greeting can make a difference in someone's day. When we choose to give of ourselves to serve others, we are giving up something (sacrifice) in order to make that happen. I think it is very important that folks get our very best when they call, go online, or walk through our doors. They, too, have worked very hard for their money as they sacrificed to get it. They deserve the best that we can give them. Let's make sure we think about the word **sacrifice** this week, and ponder on how we can make sure others see, hear, feel, get that "sacrificial" best.

That, folks, will require making a choice and effort each and every day (a commitment).

"...with the sacrifice of thanksgiving..."
—Lev. 7:12

17

"Compromising in the real world – what does it get you?"

"WE DON'T LIVE in a perfect world, we live in a real world." A big part of living in an imperfect world, I personally think, is the act of compromise. Basically, it is about people choosing what is important to them, what is of value and how they deal with the opposing side of all of that. Let's look at the definition:

1. A settlement of difference in which each side makes concessions.
2. The result of such settlement.
3. A concession to something detrimental or pejorative (a compromise of mortality).
4. To reduce the quality value or degree of something.

I have never liked the last two definitions of compromise where one has to concede for whatever the reason when the outcome will not be a future-minded decision or maybe even flat-out wrong. In other words, giving in even when you don't agree or know it is not right.

To add to this point, and to be clear, there are things we as a bank will not compromise on and those are our stacking and founding principles and character traits. The act of compromise, when not based on some principles, can get the future off on the wrong track and others not part of the compromise will have to deal with the outcome later. We can just look back on our own country's history and find countless compromises that did not work out and we are paying for still today. Compromise and outcome are other factors in a perfect vs. real world scenario.

Back to us and our daily work week. First, what do you consider to be a compromise? Is it close to the prior statements for you? Is it choosing your battles? There are some things worth giving in for that really don't matter, if it helps you get those things that really do matter. To me that is where giving in on the "doesn't matter" will help you gain ground on the "does matter". As the old saying goes, pick your battles—what is really important—shake off the rest. To me it is a way to get things rolling. Another point may be compromising with a person to avoid a confrontation? Is it what is best for all? Is all compromise good? Is all compromise bad? Have you ever compromised on something and then later regretted it and maybe paid the price for doing that? Therein lies the gray in a perfect vs. real world scenario. What if no one ever compromised on their principles? Think of those compromises that had to be made because principles were broken and earlier bad decisions were made. Do you think if folks could see years down the road the results of their actions today,would they still do those things? This is when compromise is not good for anyone, when compromise is used to cover prior bad decisions. What do you think? Does compromise bring about a more perfect or more real world?

I do think some compromise, as defined in the first definition, especially in our roles as representatives should cause us to look for what is best for others not just ourselves personally. In other words we put aside our feelings and wants for what is the best for who and what we represent and others. We have to look forward and think, is this really better for the future, not just right now? One thing we all must look at is all the facts and get a clear overall picture of what is being discussed or the direction of where we are headed on any particular decision or call. If one does not have all the pieces how can one make an accurate decision about anything? Being open minded to all the facts, seeking counsel, and giving a real study to those are critical. But once all the facts are in and you were wrong would you concede to what is right? It gets back to being fair, seeing all sides, thinking of the future, and then making the right call. In a real world hard calls must be made.

These hard calls, if made correctly, will alleviate more compromise later.

Where do we draw the line on compromise and settle for less than excellent? We must not settle for less than perfect and just say to heck with it. Let's just do that! When do we say, this is a better way for the long run and this is what works and will last? It all starts with a daily decision and focus.

"But let your statement be, 'Yes, yes or no, no'"

—Matt. 5:37

18

"It is more than a building, it is the character that counts."

I WAS VISITING with someone whom I respect. The meeting was about a significant building project that will cost in the multi-millions. This project will be something that will be totally unique and there will be nothing like it. It will hold treasures that far exceed any other museum and archives. I was reminded, and it drove home this week's thought, it is not about the building it is what the building will hold, protect, and teach to future generations, those indelible traits that no other building project can lay claim to. It is not a building project. It is far greater. It is all about unique, sacrificial character traits and values that are so lacking in our country today. If the building ever goes away, the traits that were there will be carried and live on—it is not the building, it is the people. The people who sacrificed to keep and live those traits and all those people today and tomorrow that will carry, live by and possibly pay the ultimate sacrifice for those traits.

The project I am working on was put into motion back in 1897 with the vision of Texas Ranger Captain "Rip" Ford's vision. The organization has five distinct character traits which are: **Courage, Determination, Integrity, Dedication, and Respect.** All these traits can and should be fundamental to any successful organization or company. We should take a minute and think about each and how they fit into our daily interactions with customers and each other.

Think about Courage. What if we had the courage to do the right thing all the time and speak up when something is not right? How much could we change? How many would see that and also change and do right? What examples would we set for all those that are watching who we never see? If we all practiced courage, how fast could we change the world?

Think about Determination. What if each one of us was determined (had an internal drive and passion) to exceed our goals, budgets, and customer expectations? How much better would we be? Think how much bigger we would get? How many more would move and bank with us? How many more opportunities would each of us have? How much faster, efficient, and profitable would we be if each of us was determined to be excellent in all we do? If we all practiced determination, how fast could we change the world?

Think about Integrity. This is already one of our bank's core values. One we all should be very familiar with and never cross the line on. But think what if the world we worked in had integrity and we never had to question this? We should always lead by example in integrity; it should be foremost in everything we do. As it has been said many times, everything we do should be front page newspaper worthy. If we all practiced integrity, how fast could we change the world?

Think about Dedication. What about this? What would change if all were 100 percent dedicated to the overall vision, the name, to the organization's future, our own duties, and responsibilities? If we were dedicated to all of those who pay our salaries, would they see that and be more dedicated to our bank. Dedication to me works the best when both sides are dedicated—not a one-sided way of dealing. It goes back to relationships—it reciprocates. Let others see there is "no gray" in you and give no doubts that you are dedicated. If we all practiced dedication, how fast could we change the world?

Think about Respect. To me this says it all and means all—this is the core. Without respect, there is and cannot be much to the other traits. Respect is what makes others equal. It is the equalizer. That is why no matter who, what, or where they are, every one of our customers deserves and should always be shown respect. Let's not forget they pay our salary. Respect is valuable, but in no case free. It can be lost and taken away with one's actions or lack thereof. Respect, in most cases, is also reciprocated. The showing of respect should be core in our dealings. It is that important. If we all practiced respect, how fast could we change the world?

If we were to all practice these traits every day, I promise it will set us far apart and above all the others. People will see traits in us and they will see the extra security and the value that comes with them. As I mentioned, most of these traits are reciprocated—what we plant, we will harvest. Remember one more thing, everyone is watching all the time, there are never times when no one does not see. We are on all the time, 24/7, don't forget that. We are in a business that is based on trust, integrity, and character as we deal with other's money, their hard-earned savings, their source of livelihoods and capital. It is all about reputation and perception.

These character traits are not negotiable, and they should all be what each of us practice each day. It is what our bank's name is built on. We must everyday protect, practice, and show to others we have those character traits. When the buildings are no longer around, a name based on stellar character will remain. It is more than a building, it is the character that counts.

"A good name is more desirable than great riches; to be esteemed is better than silver or gold."
—Proverbs 22:1

19

"Did you leave your mark as a good counselor this past week, and will you see the results?"

WE ALL LEAVE our mark on life and people every day, and we should take the time to reflect and see if what we said and did were the marks we really wanted to leave behind. I thought about this as I got a phone call this past Sunday morning. A mentor (TR) had passed away. A man who was not only a mentor but also a great counselor and protector. A triple dose of influence if you will. I believe that most things happen for a reason, and there are people that come and pass through one's life for reasons as well. When we moved to Gonzales, TR was one of those who walked into my life. We connected quickly and started a relationship. It did not take me long to trust him, he gained my confidence quickly. He took the time to pour into me and helped me in many ways. He was a mentor as I would watch and learn from how he handled himself, the respect he had in the community, his appearance, the skills he taught me, his solid and right-on counsel, his vigilant watch over the bank and me, and his legal advice about legal documents for loans. He always had my best interest at heart. I could never remember a time spent with TR when I did not feel good. He was a steadfast counselor for me, and I hope he could see that from me and the others he touched.

Here's one funny story to share about TR and how his ever-watchful eye worked. TR was an early riser and would leave around 5 each day. For several weeks, late each Friday before he would leave, he would call and I would hear that TR voice, which started every phone call with, "Say". He was always telling me something about a customer or something that would concern the bank in some way. There was never anything I could do about it until Monday morning though. Finally, after a few weeks of this, I told him, "TR, I really appreciate you and all you do to look out for me, but there is not a thing I can do about it until Monday, so don't tell me this anymore and make me worry about it all weekend." He laughed, and we talked on Mondays.

What do we take from this? Think, who did or does this for you? Better yet, who do you provide good counsel to? We all have an influence on others no matter what level or what position we are in. Matter of fact, I have seen folks on lower levels, throughout my career, affect a lot of higher ups. We all have that internal control, if we just use it correctly. I believe that to be of good counsel you have to have a few things to offer: skills, confidence, trust, a passion for what you are counseling on, and a rapport with whomever you're counseling. TR had all of these and he passed those on to folks like me and I am a better person because of it. I just hope TR saw in me and the others under his influence that all he taught and spoke came into fruition.

People look to us for counsel in many things, and we must do our very best because what we do affects others' lives—good or bad. Again, what we do is that important. You never know how what you say or do today will affect another's personal life or their financial outcome tomorrow. What we do can and will change others' lives as that is our business—to change lives for the better and to help others become financially successful for themselves and their families. Provide good counsel and remember you are a steward of a great legacy.

"...in the abundance of counselors there is victory."

—Proverbs 11:14

20

"When the shakin' comes – you do not have to be shaken."

WE ARE ALL familiar with the Jerry Lee Lewis hit song "Whole lot of shakin goin on" or Eddie Money's hit "Shakin'", and I am sure there are many more songs that have "shakin'" in them. The point is "shakin'" is something that is always going to happen. Shakin' is change and change is constant. There will be shakin' when we face the constant changes in life and profession. We are going through some big changes right now as we merge two large banks—there will be shakin (changes). Each one of us is going to have to change in some way and adapt, some more than others, but the deal is, we all will change. The good thing right now is we are changing as a group and this helps us bear the load. Not every change is going to sound pleasing or look like it is to our immediate benefit. When these times come, we need to stand back, let our emotions settle down, and think or even discuss what the changes will bring, finding the betterment in them. We need to make sure that emotions don't add fuel to the "shakin'". As we go through life, changes are coming faster and they are a bigger part of our daily lives. It is as if Life has excelled through the last couple of generations. I just heard this fact that the average worker today (starting in their twenties) will have seven jobs and move seven times. The better we are at adapting, the better we will be going forward. The economy, technology, innovations, tighter profit margins, consumer and investor demands, competition and other factors pull on us and our industry constantly. We need to be able to "flex" when things come our way even if we do not immediately see the good in it. Spend time in positive thought and find ways to adapt to what is going on and how to better deal with changes. I heard a very good and timely lesson on change today. The lesson dealt with unexpected life changes and the pain (unrest, being unsure of the future, and disruptions of our own plans, etc.) that goes with it.

The brunt of the lesson today was as follows: four types of pain.

1. External pain—pain that results from negative people and circumstances we encounter. The answer: seek advice and guidance.
2. Organizational pain—pain that originates from conflict in your team. The answer: be proactive.
3. Internal pain—pain that originates from our own inadequacies. The answer: be persuaded.
4. Developmental pain—pain that originates because people have to grow. The answer: be persevering.

People are always watching us and shakin' (change) invigorates that even more. People are always interested to see action or reaction. Let's show them we are solid, confident, and ready to take care of business.

"Consider it pure joy, my brothers, whenever you face trials of many kinds, because you know that the testing of your faith develops perseverance. Perseverance must finish its work so that you may be mature and complete, not lacking anything."

—James 1:2-3

21

"Breaking bread really brings it all together."

WE ALL KNOW that each of us has to eat every day to nourish our bodies to give us energy to keep going. And We all know that guacamole is one of the worst things a person cail eat (personal opinion no meaningful medical evidence that I know of to prove otherwise).

> *"Early history uses the expression 'breaking of bread' in different ways as part of their fellowship and coming together regularly for common meals, which included the breaking of bread which has been referred to as having 'everything in common'. This no doubt included sharing meals together, each one receiving from the others what they needed."*
>
> *—From Got Questions*

So, I write this as I had three "breaking bread" meals over the weekend, which spurred my thought for the week and gave me that final touch for the confirmation to write. The breaking bread with important relationships was a lunch and then two dinners. Each with folks who are close to me with a relationship built over the years. Two of the three were in the spur of the moment and the other one was a long-since planned dinner. The lunch went from a table for two to a table for four; that was cool as the four came as a surprise and it worked out to be perfect. The lunch was good food but better because of all who were seated at the table. It gave me a chance to think back to when we all first met and to see where we are today. The second was from a good friend from down South who called and wanted to get together. I could not make that time work, but quickly called back and made changes to arrange a time that we could have dinner. It was like the lunch that day was a table of four who started relationships together a few years back. It was a great time to see that all is good and nothing has changed. To not only share a reconnection, but to share in a wonderful meal and several desserts. The third was someone's thirty-fifth birthday party that I wouldn't have missed. That was a great reconnection with many other past relationships and all those folks enjoyed a good solid meal and plenty of it.

The last dinner, the birthday party, I almost missed, after planning it for months and driving two-and-a-half hours to get to it. We had gone south earlier in the day so I could get a round of brush spraying in before the party. That led to getting a tractor stuck to the axles and then an effort on my part to pull the tractor out. Got my truck stuck to the axles as well. My uncle came over from his place and could not get us out, so my dad called a cousin who borders my dad's farm and whom I have never met. He showed up, added more links of chain, and said to say a Chevy pulled a Ford out of a bad way. So, when I offered to pay him for getting me out of a pickle, he said nothing needed paying. I said, "Maybe we can have you over and cook for you?" Then my dad said, "We will have you over to break bread." So, we will do that with a relative I've never met before to get the opportunity for connection.

Breaking bread is more than just a way to fill your stomach, it is a time to show how you value and appreciate the relationship.

We all have to take time to show others sincere appreciation for their relationship. There will be times when we get to break bread at a dinner table and then there will be times we can grab a coffee and a cookie. Your future, your success, your thought life, and your daily decision. Think about it.

'"Finally…whatever is true, whatever is honorable, whatever is right, whatever is pure…whatever is of good repute…let your mind dwell on these things."
—Phil. 4:8

22

"How many things get missed or shortened when others don't speak up?"

LAST WEEK, KIM, Melyn, and I stopped by to get a quick supper at What-a-Burger. As we walked in, Kim got sidetracked with someone she knew and asked me to order for her. I went up and ordered her special #1 with mustard, mayonnaise, grilled onions, and jalapenos—all the way. Melyn ordered her special and then I ordered my patty melt. Melyn and I sat down, and Kim joined us, asking if I had ordered her dinner and done so correctly. I gave her a definitive "yes, I did". So, the three of us visited until our meal came. The order came and I handed off the hamburgers and fries, like a dealer deals a stack of cards. Kim unwrapped her hamburger and took her first bite and the first words out were not "thank you" or anything like that. The words started with my middle initial. She opened the hamburger and saw there was no cheese. As Melyn started to laugh and Kim was "visiting" with me about forgetting that item (this is not the first time I have gotten this wrong). I quickly shifted the direction to the wait staff at the counter. My response was, if she would have asked, "do you want cheese on that," as they are trained to do, I would have said yes. Of course, Kim did not buy that or my lack of attention to detail. I told this story at leadership this week as we discussed a point that made this relevant. We can laugh as Melyn did and think it was funny, which it was. But there is a point to this story, a story that happens every day when a trained salesperson does not do their job. See, in this example, not only did What-a-Burger miss a sale on a high profit item, it also made the customer experience less. All the clerk had to ask was, "Do you want to add cheese, up the drink size, dessert, or anything else?", close the sale, then say the two most important words: "Thank you."

Pretty simple, but yet it is missed all the time by many, many people. You wonder, "Why did they not do that?"

The above example is not the first for us and, I am sure, everyone reading can name dozens of examples of both sales and even from professionals who did not ask the right questions or help improve the experience. I think sometimes the customer forgets the basics as I did with the cheese because I was focused on getting all the other extras in. A basic item that someone has always asked to add. Missing cheese on a hamburger is not going to have a major impact, but it does lessen the overall experience. Especially when you were geared up with a set expectation of what the taste was going to be like. What if it were a bigger deal? What if it had a financial impact? I think these little things are what separate the average service from superb service—that little extra service that adds to the overall experience. The person who pays attention to the details that bring value and maybe things that a customer might have forgotten or not even known about. As I said, hamburgers are one thing, but what about things that have to do with financial products and services?

Dealing with someone's livelihood and finances is not only about today, but it is really about the future, and this is much bigger than cheese on a hamburger. The future brings a greater responsibility and this is where being a true professional really changes things. Things that should be part of our daily duty to all that we come in contact with. Think about what a doctor does when you are sitting in front of him and what he asks as he searches for the right cure to find out the real reason you are there. He is not asking questions to sell things the pharmaceutical rep just left on his desk. He is really trying to solve the need, the same as what we should be doing. That is bringing and adding value to every customer experience (transactions and requests), building lifetime relationships and always looking for the very best for the future. It all starts with being ready, being proactive, doing our best, asking the right questions, and bringing the expertise, initiative, and passion for excellence.

Being a professional is doing everything right, plus addressing all those extra intangibles that will be required in the future.

"...and I show you a still more excellent way."

—1 Cor. 12:31

23

"Some people bring out the little extra that makes your job really special"

KIM AND I have been very fortunate to have moved around Texas and experienced a lot of different things. Each move has brought us a new season in life, which has allowed us to build our life skills and get us to where we are today. Probably the best part of us moving around has been all the people we've met and developed a relationship with. We have learned a tremendous amount from most of these folks and about life in general—it has prepared Kim and me for things to come and made us better folks.

This weekend, Kim and I went back to Gonzales to pay our last respects to one of those who influenced us. Kim grew up in Gonzales, so she knew folks and that got us started when we moved there. The rest was up to us with what to do with those relationships and how to bring in new ones. One of those new relationships was our neighbor. She was really something. Kim loved her because she was honest and everyone knew where they stood with her and, more importantly, where she stood. She was self-made and all Texan. She was raised ranching and farming, loved and appreciated her land, and knew the value of a dollar. She went to work at an early age, but decided to get an education, going to Teacher College. Getting her certificate, she taught for years. Again, a common bond with Kim. One of the things we remember about her was that little red light (end of a cigarette) we could see from her back porch. When we would see that, we would head over and would sit and talk with her about her growing up, teaching, banking rates, and Gonzales history and politics (i.e., talk about other folks). She would tell Melyn, "You have to kiss a lot of frogs to find the right one." She gave Melyn a ceramic frog that Melyn keeps in her room. One funny story was the day she called me at the bank and told me to come home and shoot a possum that had something wrong with it. When I got home, I saw it walking in circles in our back alley. I called the police and told them I was going to fire a .22 in town, but the possum kept walking in circles and up against a curb. So, not to get a ricochet off the curb, I popped him with a shotgun which was a little louder than a .22. I picked up the possum and put him in the trash can—a good deed done. That afternoon, a neighbor asked me about the lunch-time shooting. I told them something was wrong with an animal, so I had to shoot it. Well, I found out why. The neighbor had hit it in the head with a baseball bat, thus the reason for the delirious walk. In other words, it was not rabid. It was just one of the animals I "took care" of for her.

One of the neat things about these relationships is that they cross over because she was also a bank customer. She would always try to get the best deal and remind me what the other banks were paying. She was a real joy to deal with and a pleasure to have as a customer. She made my job better. I would really look forward to having her in the bank. That is one of the very unique things about banking as you can really develop strong relationships with folks that crossed both personal and business lines. It is what makes banking such a fulfilling career. The people are the best part of our jobs. The relationship is what it is all about. Having someone call you their banker is about as high a compliment as one in our field can ever hope to get.

Every day we should develop and strengthen relationships, so we can maximize all that a true banking relationship can bring forth. If we can just get others to think of us as their bankers, we keep the other banks out of our neighborhood.

"To everything there is a season and time for every purpose under Heaven."

—Ecc. 3:1

24

"Build rapport, so when you need it, it is there"

RAPPORT AS DEFINED in Webster's: "*Rapport is one of the most important features or characteristics of human interaction. It is a commonality of perspective, being in 'sync', being on the same wavelength as the person you are talking to. Achieving rapport with someone may come naturally, but it may not. There may be good chemistry, there may not. If you are having difficulty, then the way to establish rapport is to enter the world view of the other person, to accept their view of the world. Moreover there are subtle techniques you can use such as matching body posture, maintaining eye contact, and matching breathing rhythm. Some of these techniques are explored in neurolinguistic programming, a branch of psychology. If rapport is established, then instead of being out of step with the other person, you are in step. You find that you have built a foundation for a more effective give-and-take relationship. Your point of view receives more generous consideration."*

Having rapport is extremely important as this is something way beyond the deal. I was very fortunate to attend a national leadership summit where this topic was taught, and it is huge. The above definition only begins to cover the depth of what rapport is. It is beyond the paperwork, let's not forget the paperwork. Keeping the records straight allows for the accountability to be tracked and keeps everything "legal." I have heard it said that "there is nothing I can't talk my way out of". This is what I meant partly with my "thought of the week." There are communication and personal connections that must be made. What common ground can you find with another that builds the bridge, fills the gap, provides the needed trust, confidence, and, generally, that magical commonality that bonds folks together?

I think we need to develop a rapport with others so that when things do not work out as planned there are options. Think about this, have you ever not liked someone when there were no problems? Then, you were forced to deal with them when there was a problem? How did that go? Did you really look for a solution? A win-win on both sides? Or did you just look for a way out, demand your way, give in or just walk away? No rapport—no solution for both sides.

Now think about a relationship where you really enjoyed the other person to the point where you would not mind if the other side won or got more than their fair share. Think about what would happen if something came up with the relationship. I would say that would be less stressful and the outcome would be much easier to overcome and more than likely a win-win.

This is my point about building rapport for when you need it. It's so important in our positions as bankers. We deal with the cash flow (lifeblood) of most households and companies. We need to take the opportunities to reach out and solidify the relationship before issues pop up or, more importantly, someone else steps in our place. Don't we want folks to come to us because they know we take care of them and they feel comfortable with us? Rapport building begins with you extending your hand, and allowing others the freedom to approach you. It's also making yourself adjust and fit in with the customer's element. I think sometimes we have to be somewhat of a chameleon, so we can adapt and become part of the environment and not make the customers feel they have to always adapt. Sometimes, it is simply being liked and enjoyed by others. You find a way to common ground. You are not a threat or part of the problem but the fit and the solution. Rapport is more than just being friendly, it is adapting and showing your desire to fit. It makes a difference being a part of the solution, building confidence and trust.

I've found it true to have been able to present my case, talk through my positions and even work through some tight spots with someone I've built rapport with. I've also been in the same spot when I did not have a rapport with the customer and the two have not always worked out the same. An easier way to look at this is favor—you either have it or not.

"...favor is like a cloud with the spring rain."
—Proverbs 15:15

25

"Commencement means to start–not to end"

I ATTENDED TWO graduations this weekend and watched a lot of young people walk across the stage. It made me think about these young folks and what they have ahead of them. Twelve years of learning and the daily grind to get them to one night. To some it means they will start the work world, to others military and to some more education and skills. All together for one last night then they all go their own ways. It is funny how you see folks for twelve years, get to know them, then it happens, that season is over and a new season of life starts. Some will stay close and others will never see each other again. That is why we have commencement services. The definition of which is 1. The time at which something is to begin, 2. An academic exercise, 3. The act of starting something. Commencement is forward, not backward, not resting, not thinking about what you have accomplished or done. Maybe a better phrase is the firing line quote: "Commence firing," in other words, "pull the trigger and throw lead."

Take a few minutes to think back to your graduation(s). What were you thinking then and what directions were you headed? Did you ever think you would be where you are today? Personally, I would have never thought that I would one day live in Kingsville and have the unique opportunity and privilege to work for Kleberg Bank, even when I was writing my high school research paper on the King Ranch. To further that, I never would have considered at the time that I would have a daughter and she would graduate from the junior high on the King Ranch proper. I wouldn't have thought I'd have a wife that teaches for the King Ranch School. You just never know what treasures life will bring to you, but you better be ready and willing to move (commence) when these rare opportunities present themselves.

Do you remember all those that were there that commencement day and those that are now gone? Do you remember those that taught you life lessons and mentored you? Did you think of commencement as a new start and a new life for you on your own? Were you ready? Did you know what you wanted to be and do? I knew, for me, there were two paths I would have to choose from. To me, once the decision or commitment was made, there was no time to waste and college needed to be a one-time deal with no do-overs. Get it knocked out and go to work. Once banking was chosen it was my focus from then through today.

We live in a very unique time, work for a bank like no other and have great opportunities to influence and help others as they walk across the stage of life. Think about that for a moment, and the seasons of life in general. A bank is a very big part of one's life and those seasons. Think about a young person's needs and how they can change over time, from the first car loan to the first home, to the "I need to fix up the home" loan, to the "next size up" home, then maybe a second home, then all the business loans from "I am ready to start" to "I'm ready to expand my vision and put more to work". Then we have all the others: "I need help in planning my retirement, save for my kids' college, and I want to leave behind something for those yet to come." What we do is very important.

We need to be the ones who help others commence and go forward in life by providing the best in banking and financial services that will ensure their dreams and visions become reality. We should take pride knowing we make the difference.

"...and your young men shall see visions."
—Acts 2:17

26

"Sometimes we take little things like central HVAC for granted."

I WONDER HOW many of us think about the comfort and convenience that a modern central air conditioning and heating unit system provide? Do many of us give that a second thought as we enter a building? I thought about this early the other morning when I opened the bank. That morning was very cool and a little damp. Maybe the scurrying across the parking lot in the cold to get to the door and inside the warm building spurred the thought, but it hit me just as sure as the warm air did that this modern day convenience is one we all, I think, take for granted and many, including me, at times don't give second thought to.

I can still remember vividly, and I know many of you would find this hard to believe, but I went all through public school including Senior High School without air conditioning. Yes, we had a whopping two corner fans mounted on opposing walls in each class room—you know that was way more than needed. You would not want too much comfort or air circulation as that might cause unrest among the population. Yes, all outside windows were open for those brave souls who could slip out and run around and slip back into class without being noticed. So the incentive to getting to class on time or early was you could reach up and redirect the fan and get more air on your row. And yes it was for the benefit of the entire class—not! It was a benefit to those that got there early. This gets me on the subject of that same time in sports when we would have two-a-day football practice and we'd only get one water break with a small cup. Today, if you don't stop every five minutes to drink a gallon of water, sirens goes off—that is a whole other topic.

During my high school years I also spent a lot of time in attics installing HVAC units in both new and old houses that were being updated as well. I have many stories on those experiences and lots of funny and "HOT!" memories to go with it. As those were in old houses with no ventilation at all, old attics, rockwall fiberglass insulation (that would stick in your skin and itch all night), darkness, with plenty of roofing nails to tap your head on all in the middle of the summer in the nice warm Gulf Coast. So, I have a rather unique perspective of a time when HVAC was still not as common and prolific as it is today. Installing and being on many service calls of those whose units went out has given me an appreciation for what we have today.

Again, when I walked into our beautiful hill country, custom-built bank building and all temperatures were perfect, it made me reflect. It made me think back on when you had to control temperatures, someone had to be there early to start the units or turn on a furnace to get everything warmed up a few hours before the start of the day. All we do now is walk in and everything is ready and running. "Times, they are a changing" as the song says.

You know as soon as the above thoughts hit me and I had time to reflect, the next thing that was clear to me was beyond just a comfortably heated bank, but it was on a more personal relationship level. It was the thought: do we all do what we can to set the right climate for all who enter our doors? Do we have the thermostat set so that everyone that walks in feels comfortable? In other words, from a more important "personal climate" standpoint, do our customers and guests feel wanted, appreciated, respected, valued, and given full attention? Are they being taken care of so they walk out fully satisfied, with their needs met? Is their personal temperature rating (thermostat) set so, when they walk out, they tell everyone about how comfortable our bank is?

Let's not take the HVAC or the thermostat we all control for granted—we need to ensure everyone we touch walks away with a perfect temperature setting.

"Therefore do not fear, you are of more value."
—Matt. 10:31

27

"There is nothing pro in procrastination."

THINK ABOUT THIS "proactive crastination" (dictionary definition of crastination: putting off until tomorrow). When you say it that way it sounds a little more real and not so good. It is almost an oxymoron. Being in an action state of mind to make a decision not to do something until later… maybe? A conscious decision not to react, so, in other words, proactively not reacting. I think we are all guilty of some sort of procrastination, some more than others. There is a whole array of issues and excuses that cause us to delay. It may be something we just dread doing, it may be a tough call, something that causes us to stress a bit or makes us uneasy to say the least. But, does delaying make it better? Does it make it worse by deliberately avoiding the inevitable? I think everyone deals with procrastination in different ways, but all end up in the same spot. Nothing gets done and the task at hand is still there waiting. The bad thing is sometimes, on second

thought, many times, the issue just gets a whole lot worse with the passing of time.

The other thing about procrastination is the other party (the "procrastinee") is the one that gets the short end of the stick. The "procrastinator" usually does not realize the stress and questioning state of mind that the procrastinee has been in while waiting for an answer or the results to come to pass. We have to know that others depend on us, and that others either increase their confidence in us or everything that blocks their satisfaction or expectations decreases that confidence. Procrastination lessens our best and lessens others' confidence in us. We must not allow procrastination to be an issue for it is an enemy of excellent service, and for us to exceed customer expectations, it has to be overcome at all costs. Think about this example, if you really needed something shipped and you were relying on somebody else to take care of that. Let's say you needed a part for your car to be drivable. You were on foot without it. You call back to the auto parts and it has been three days and the person you thought had ordered your part had yet to do so. What would you think and how would you react?

Would you just skip to work and whistle or would you call another auto parts store and never go back to the first? We cannot procrastinate, we are in a competitive world and, more importantly, our customers

deserve more than time delays and less-than-best efforts.

So, we must do the uncomfortable, face the issues that we would rather not deal with, manage our time better, and become more efficient. Stop the delays and the easy distractions that give us a way out or an excuse. Prioritization is a must. The first thing I do every morning is make a list on a yellow pad of what I need to do. Does it work? Sometimes, there are constant distractions daily to deal with. If you can't get to something, you should always let others know you can't make a deadline or meet their expectations. The yellow pad is a kind of accountability tracking sheet. Another enemy of procrastination is communication. If you practice good communication, it puts you in a position of accountability and it helps push you and the task along. One other big thing about procrastination is lost opportunity. How many opportunities get lost every day to waiting, hindrances, and just not reacting? I would guess thousands of opportunities , some never return again.

Watch yourself this week, really think about your daily list of "must get done today" items—no excuses. Avoid the easy way out and the distractions. Do you really need to spend time on that right now? Can that wait?

Can you do something more productive? Watch the clock, so to speak, and see if, at a certain time, you are where you need to be. Time is money, and we are in a business where not only is our time costly, but our customer's time is as well. We need to make every workday count and breaking it down is a good way to self-monitor during the day. Check your list and mark off those things that you get down and continue focusing on the others. We have all heard of the time value of money, so if we flip that, we can say that money is time and the better we use it the more money should be generated. We must be diligent in all our efforts—all the time.

"Watch over your heart with all diligence."

—Proverbs 4:23

28

"Spoken words and actions create memories that last."

WE ALL HAVE memories and some are great, some are good, and, yes, some are not good, and there are all variations in between.

Before you read this thought, please take the time to think of a strong memory and think about why it had such an impression on you. Does that memory drive your behaviors today? Memories defined are 1. the mental capacity of retaining facts, events, impressions of previous experiences, 2. to draw from memory, 3. the length of time within the memory of living persons, 4. a mental impression retained. I shortened the definitions to what I think is important for today's thought. Memories are extremely important, and they determine a lot of what will happen as they are lasting drivers that impact our futures. Think about that, what do you do or don't do today that is spurred by memories of prior experiences of spoken words or actions by others and, yes, even ourselves?

A few memory quotes to consider: "We do not remember days, we remember moments." —Cesare Pavese, *The Burning Brand*. This is true, I don't remember the day, I remember the driving life event itself. Those are the events of which I can remember every little detail—the spoken words, actions, and every little aspect surrounding them. It is like a movie that is ready to be played in full color with surround sound. Like the day Melyn was born and still hearing the doctor, seeing the exact layout of the room, and meeting Melyn for the very first time. It is still crystal clear. Yes, I remember the disappointments that life brings as well and all those movies play just as clear and loud. I think, in part, why those stick in your brain is those times are so emotionally charged that you are super sensitive. All your senses and faculties are 100 percent engaged and in maximum capacity, adding to the moment.

"Memory is a way of holding onto the things you love, the things you are, the things you never want to lose." —From the television show "The Wonder Years". Great TV show by the way and captures a time when I was growing up. It was so true. Think about the times you loved that are no longer here. Think how those memories are still strong and can even carry you still today. Think about what you do to perpetuate and protect those memories. Think about why folks have all those pictures around? Why do we pay photographers to take professional pictures? Why do we find ourselves taking pictures? It is so we can capture that moment and hold on to it. We capture those for safe keeping—we keep a record of that event—that time and that exact moment in our life.

"The past is never dead, it is not even past."—William Faulkner. This is the exact point of my thought today. The past, in some respects, never really is dead and it is as alive as the day, hour, minute, and second it happened. That memory is driving today and it may never change or create a new direction.

Here is my point, I was talking to someone about the bank this weekend in a relaxed conversation. But it got real direct, and all thanks to a memory. A bad memory, unfortunately, that happened many years ago with folks who are no longer here. It is the reason they are not banking with us today. Since those memory creators are no longer here, we will create new memories. This is not the first time I've experienced this. I can remember years ago, at another bank, I was asking a man to move over. His response was he was turned down from and would not be coming back. This man was in his mid-eighties and that probably happened fifty to sixty years ago. The person who'd declined it has been dead for years and that bank has changed names three times. But the day I asked him to bank with us, to him, it was as alive as the day it happened.

Folks, we may only have one chance to make an impression and create a customer for life. The experiences we create are not about us, they're about this institution. The examples I gave were personal experiences with clients who are no longer with the bank, and in that case the institution suffered and lost. So, always think about this institution and how you represent something bigger. It is 1000 percent up to us individually and collectively every day.

Every day we must treat everyone with respect and dignity. In an utmost professional manner, we must always say thank you and show great appreciation. This is paramount. Think before you speak or act, think of how you would like what you are about to say or do.

What if it was done to you? If you would not like it, consider that before acting. We personally and collectively create memories every day. We want to create memories by our spoken words and actions that will be so powerful and forward moving that they will provide future growth benefiting all—if not, the other will happen and we all lose, it is as simple as that.

Create memories that allow us to build with pride everyday. Let's leave good memories, memories that allow good things for all those coming behind us.

"The memory of the righteous is blessed."
—Proverbs 10:7

29

"Sometimes the timing has to be just right."

OVER THE YEARS, I have worked hard, thought ahead, planned for things, and driven down certain highways in life. There, as we all know very well, are curves, unexpected detours, and chug holes that lie in every road. You just have to watch the road, make adjustments, and avoid all you can. Keep the dents and flat tires out altogether or to a minimum and keep on going. No stopping to look back or pulling over to overthink about it, just adjust, keep your foot on the gas pedal, and roll forward. I can still remember a few bank deals that were a disappointment at the time but turned out a whole lot better later. One in particular was a large municipal bond project I did not get the first time and was pretty bummed about it, but I kept the doors open wide and was able to get it on the second round at a much better offering. There have been other life experiences that have turned out the same way. That does not mean you don't try hard or give in or up —it just means, when things don't work out, you keep looking for other ways around, keep focused on the end results (attitude right), have your eyes wide open to get to where you want to be, and keep looking for new opportunities.

This past weekend, something finally happened that I really wanted over seven years ago. It was a true gift to me to see it finally come to fruition. It was not a normally wrapped present but it was an opportunity to meet someone and have an event that he would be a part of. It was on my "bucket list". I have always wanted to meet Johnny Rodriguez (for you who do not know Mr. Rodriguez, use "modern technology" and Google him) and, about seven years ago, I wanted to have him for an event Kim and I were working on and planning. The timing was not right, but even then I had it in my mind exactly how I wanted the event to play out, who would be there, what would occur, and what would be said. Skip forward to this past weekend at an event with the same organization, and it finally happened. The host was just as excited about having him as I was planning to get the singer for our event. I was elated for the host, as we both shared this event vision and enthusiasm as he made it happen in another time and place.

This was a big deal as I was looking forward to it for the reasons I mentioned above. I can still remember where I was as a kid, when I first heard stories of how the singer was discovered and who discovered him. I grew up listening to his music, never thinking I would meet or be with him at an event. Kim and I had met the Ranger who discovered him years before and I always thought it would be really something to have those two people together and that was part of my event plan. Right before the concert, Kim and I were standing with the Ranger, and I heard Kim say, "There he is". Sure enough, there was Johnny Rodriguez walking up. I handed him the gift I bought for him at the Saddle Shop and told him I have waited a long time to meet him. We got our picture taken with him, the Ranger and the host. I thought about what I had planned before and asked the host if the Ranger could introduce him and tell the complete detailed story. It happened and it is now recorded (part of History) how a Texas Ranger discovered Johnny Rodriguez and helped him start his music career. I sat back and watched intensely and enjoyed every minute of this as it finally happened after all those years.

This week, as they say, "timing is everything." It really is, and I have learned that to be truer the older

I get. I believe firmly that things happen for a reason. Again, that does not mean you don't do your part because I also believe things happen for a reason when you are doing your part. Life is not easy, and it takes hard work and daily diligence to get to where we need to be as an institution, and individually as well. It takes all of us doing our parts 110 percent to the best of our ability. When things don't go the first time don't stop—keep in pursuit—keep pressing forward. Nothing gets done on its own, someone has to make it happen and that needs to be every one of us. As the old adage goes, when at first you don't succeed, try, try again. Sometimes, the second and third tries turn out so much better. We need to be tenacious, expeditious, and diligent in all we do daily. Strive to excel and exceed.

"There is an appointed time for everything..."

—Ecc. 3:1

30

"Enjoy the journey."

THIS WAS TOLD to me this past week by another manager—actually twice. Like all my thoughts for the week, it was something that made me think and reflect. For years, I have been writing thoughts that started off as shorter quick points of something that was pressing and needed to be reiterated again. The thoughts were related to either an issue that arose or in some cases personnel matters that needed to be addressed. In most cases a "shot across the bow" was a good reminder to all. As some were a hint to the wise, others were "self-medicating", a chance to write maybe even a personal note to myself, something that needed to be put on paper for later reflection. All are being compiled in a book that I will leave behind one day for Melyn. I see every chance to write about an issue as a lesson or instruction for her and all those yet to come, some I will never see. This was one of those thoughts.

"Enjoy the journey", I have had a paying job since I was fourteen and have been working ever since. It is something that was instilled in me early on by my dad and grandfather. As I grew up, I found myself being mentored and drawn to those who were hard-working, self-made men who had strong work ethics at their cores. All of them just flat out worked hard, and it drove them. None of them ever had to have someone motivate them, remind them to do their jobs, or have to check on them. They all would manage themselves. Things got done and decisions were made in their world. They all enjoyed it as it was who they were and most owned and operated their own businesses, so all they did added value to their families. Something each of them will or did leave behind.

This goes back to my thought last week on "build" and that vision the bank was started on. It is something that I was geared early on for, and I have really enjoyed doing it. Even the things I do outside the bank some see as work too. If we are all working on doing the right things productively for the future, we build upward. The above comment was made to me by a person who knows me well and I have a tendency to focus on future. It is not uncommon for me to catch myself thinking five or ten plus years down the road and as for all the how, where, and whens. Many days, I wake up thinking and driving to work focused on "down the road". I think that is healthy as we all need to have a vision for the road ahead. "Enjoy the journey" was a reminder to enjoy the road and the travel time. Just as driving down the road may not always be the most exciting and best use of time, the road time is necessary, so we might as well enjoy the ride while we're in the car. I found that is a good time to read and catch up on emails and phone calls (tongue in cheek).

My point this week is, "enjoy the journey". None of us know the number of days we have, and each day is a gift. As we meet and take care of customers and solicit prospects, we need to keep that in mind. We need to make their journey with us as enjoyable as possible and give them the respect and value they deserve for being a part of Kleberg Bank. We need to take the gray out, carry the load, and make banking with us easy and allow them to enjoy their personal journeys more than before they walked into our locations. If you are thinking about your future, don't you want others thinking of yours as well and helping you get to where you want to be? That is exactly what we can and should do for everyone else.

If we will just do what we are supposed to in an excellent way each day, it will allow us as well as others to not only "enjoy their journey", but to build a solid future that is both worthy and deserving to have. It takes each of us working hard and leading the way to get there.

"Let us take our journey and go,
and I will go before you."
—Gen. 33:12

31

"I fully acknowledge my time is very valuable and it is limited."

WE ALL SHOULD say this to ourselves a few times before reading on. Put yourself in this quote and see it as the most important thing and you can have an impact over each day. Time is a constantly decreasing variable in life.

The clock never quits, always ticking away. It has no favorites and no one escapes its constantly moving hands. Everyone is equal. I believe time is entrusted to us to make things happen, not to waste. Time is something you cannot get back, and once it is gone you have nothing but regret. This is a very important point to ponder.

Think about this, if time is limited and you wasted the time you had to complete a task, where does the time come from to complete the task you still have open? It comes from your future time. The future time you had for new things now gets eaten up with wasted time from the time that has already passed. Not only do you waste your (and others') appropriated time but you waste time that can be spent on new endeavors. It really gets back to the old adage of wasted opportunity costs. Wasted time costs you opportunities.

The above not only affects you—but it greatly affects others. I know we have all needed something from someone else on a deadline and we were totally dependent on them to deliver. What did that feel like? What did you feel like when the time came for you to get whatever you needed and it was not there? What happens when others wait and they do not get what they need? What happens to all the others that rely on them downstream? We really may never know how many get affected by someone's lack of action, promptness, or production of what was needed at the time. Anyone who wastes time and does not deliver wastes others time and it costs others money and opportunities. Are you known for being that type of person?

Time is money as we all know. But our business brings this fact to reality. The basis of banking is based on the clock. The number one cost and the number one revenue is based on interest. Interest is the ultimate time value of money. Interest never stops. Interest is not a five day and eight-to-five calculation, it does not stop to take a break, visit, or get distracted. Interest is always on time and it is consistent. It ticks away and adds up all the time. Our cost keeps adding every day and we must be very aware that we need to be bringing in loans and services to offset those costs. We do this by being prompt, responsive, and turning loan and service requests quickly into an income stream. This does not happen when we do not get our work out on time or have loans go unbooked. It does not happen when we make mistakes or send in incomplete work that takes others time to address. Every day we miss an opportunity to book a loan or add a service we lost a day to offset the constant interest expenses. We can control revenue and this we must do to our very best. But it all starts with maximizing our time. If we fail to maximize our time, we cannot maximize the interest addition. As interest ticks so does our hourly payroll, so we must all be diligent with our time. Do this at the end of a day each week, figure out what you make a day and see if you covered your paycheck. Furthermore, see if you prevented someone else from making their paycheck by giving them errors to correct or holding up their time in other areas.

Think about this: does what I am doing provide excellence in service or is it making profits? If not, you probably should stop and focus on what does.

Time is money, but most importantly time is life itself—no one should waste it.

"There is an appointed time for everything."

—Ecc 3:1

32

"A surprise may be good for a birthday party, but not much else."

THIS PAST VETERAN'S Day, I was out working in our pastures before coming in for lunch and flipping on the TV. Being, of course, Veteran's Day, war movies were on and the one I started to watch was Tora! Tora! Tora! The movie was about the surprise attack on Pearl Harbor. I saw this movie years ago, but what really got my attention this time was the amount of signs, warnings, and actual sightings that were not acted upon, which led to a huge surprise and the loss of many lives. A few of the warnings started off as hunches (this does not look right) and then developed into supported intelligence. It started with one officer in DC, who was watching communications (his job was to look for warnings, things that did not look right, and gather intelligence that would need to be addressed) from the Japanese Embassy and other sources of communications. These initial reports were taken but nothing happened. Later, the same person found hard supporting evidence, but it was too late because many of the decision makers were not available. They did not take the lead and one even refused to make the call to Hawaii as he was trying to decide to call someone higher up. Finally, at the last thirty minutes, the same officer connected with the decision maker and an approved message was taken to the communications department. Even then there were further delays. There was even a sighting and a US military firing on a submarine entering the harbor. This report was dismissed as a "rookie getting excited". Then the radar station on the island picked up a large squadron of airplanes coming in. That call was unheeded by the command center as everyone was gone except one lieutenant who told them to not worry about it, that it was probably a group of planes coming in from the mainland. Overall, many folks dropped the ball and many did not react and those who did were too late. What if Pearl Harbor had a week's notice of the pending attack? What if they would have sounded that alarm when the airplanes were picked up on radar? What would a thirty minute warning have done? How many of our planes would have been airborne and ready to fight? How many gunners would have been on deck ready to fire when they came in? A surprise came that day, December 7, 1941. A day when a few were doing their jobs and others struggled with communication, skepticism, and procrastination. We can fast forward to that tragic day of 9/11/01, when again a surprise came.

We do not deal in life and death, but we do deal in serious financial matters. We all have the duty of having "no surprises" come to any of us, our customers, or our bank. That takes all "having our head in the game". We need to be doing our best at our positions, bringing to light issues, asking questions, clarifying confusion, and listening to those "this doesn't feel right" gut instincts. There are so many moving parts in the world today, we must be very diligent to always look out and be the protectors of our bank and customers. That means not only risks and anything that can create problems but also good opportunities that we or our customers do not want to miss. Either way, no surprises means we all have to buy in, speak up, and make sure all who need to listen are doing so and reacting to the message. We can, in most cases, fix anything if we all know about it as soon as something happens. If we don't know, then the results are not as good. That is when the surprise factor comes in.

Time, preparation, and having a back-up plan are all enemies of surprise. Being proactive is better than all of those. Be ever diligent, always think about risk management. That means all. The whats that could go wrong, the what-ifs, and the what-coulds? If so, we can mitigate, react, fix, or correct. Thinking and planning before something happens usually prevents anything from happening in the first place.

"...let it be carried out with all diligence."

—Ezra 6:12

33

"Producing chickens is a time-sensitive, hard push that we need to relate to our world."

THIS PAST WEEKEND was our first round of culling chickens for the upcoming livestock show. As I awoke early Sunday morning, thinking about what to write this week, chickens were on my mind, my past experiences with chickens and how this all relates to us in banking. One thing that made me think about the banking comparison is that chickens process their consumed feed every two hours, so you better be out there getting them to eat. Just like us, about 25 percent of our loan portfolio rolls (not including deposits that move up and down as well) off every year and that equates to replacing those and adding new loans. Raising chickens is all about pushing a bird to grow (put the weight on), but in a manner that does so without stressing the bird. Constant diligence is needed because they require overall monitoring and care. It is all about time value and protection from all sorts of outside forces.

I grew up raising capons (steer chickens) and did so from grammar school through high school. I made the show every year except one, when predators tore into our cage and we had capons strung out all over our yard. I saved money each year and ended up with enough money to buy Kim's wedding ring years later from all that work. After getting into banking we moved to Gonzales, which is one of the top chicken producing.counties in the state, as well as top cow calf producer (put that one in for Jim so I won't have to hear about that later). Having a little background knowledge in chickens helped.

There is a lot to raising a four-pound range bird in a little over a month. The growers that can produce make money and the ones that don't... don't. They all get paid on a competitive pay scale. It takes hard work pushing the birds and monitoring all the risks associated with doing so. On the production side, every day you cut out, reach the weight limit, and get to the processing plant is pure cash money. There are significant daily costs (feed is the #1 factor) and the conversion rate gets less as the birds get older. You would be amazed at what taking one day off of a poultry run can do to the bottom line of a poultry company—it is huge. Outside the basic daily production focus are all the other outside factors that you have to stay on guard for. This is where the stories get long, so I will give just a few examples. These have to do with the constant diligence, monitoring, and protection. For the company there are all sorts of competitive pressures from the overall international protein market issues, other poultry producers (pricing and production volumes), and governmental factors. Outside factors are, for one, diseases that can wipe out an entire poultry house and set quarantines. This actually happened and a nationwide quarantine occurred due to one lone producer who brought in poultry diseases to Gonzales. Regulating the temperature in Texas can be a challenge as well, there have been entire houses that have lost their entire chicken flocks because the thermometers and curtain systems (some of the human error) failed. Then you have the occasional poultry truck highway rollover in the rain that causes your local banker to leave his desk and pick up chickens on the side of the highway. Yes, those things happen and you have to pitch in—it is that add value mantra.

So, how does producing chickens relate to us? 1. It is all about production—the understanding of the conversion rates (the time-sensitive value of money, getting loans produced, and all the growing, serving, and providing all types of services). 2. Monitoring—the constant diligence, monitoring, and protection. That is the daily vigilance over our customer accounts and ensuring that all we are doing is providing the very best service and care they all deserve. Protecting them and the bank from all outside factors that would interrupt the goal of providing excellence in all we do.

We all need to produce daily in an excellent manner, be diligent in all things, and be ever mindful of everything around us. We need to add value to our customer's lives. We need to earn our keep.

"...for the laborer is worthy of his wages."
—Luke 10:7

34

"Accuracy matters as it does not just affect you but others."

NUMBERS AND SCORES matter. They keep account of many things and tell the story. Accurate records count for more than most give thought to on a daily basis. This thought was spurred by a few things out of the bank—one being an FFA banquet I attended at TIVY. I still remember some of the officer position statements and some of the Creed. It brought back a memory of something I did not accomplish and regretted. It was my Lone Star State Farmer pin. I had done everything I needed to do except keep my record book on my agriculture project. I've thought many times over why in the heck did I not keep up with that book and turn it in to get

the last rank in the FFA. So, what do I do growing up in a house headed by an accountant? I get an accounting degree and keep good books going forward. Numbers matter and accurate and complete numbers are key.

I can tell many stories in banking and general life events that were affected greatly by numbers, some success stories and others "not so good" stories. Those stories where the lack of numbers or inaccurate numbers gave bad results. I can also think back on competitive situations outside of the bank when teams I have been on had the records kept wrong or left off scores, thus allowing others to step ahead into the winner's circle. Being just a little bit competitive, that did not sit well with me at all. Again, not keeping up with records, not tracking numbers, and being inaccurate not only affects the person tracking but impacts those on the receiving end. The third parties that had given all the effort, but because of the lack of concern, oversight, or double checking lost out.

Being accurate matters in most all things. I have heard it said in my prior life by others that we are not in the brain surgery or life-and-death business. We may not be, but that does not allow for mediocracy or slackness. Being accurate is that important. For example, in shooting, the slightest tip of the muzzle will be a hit or a miss down range. That little initial movement really magnifies down range. Just as any slight error or a misspoken word on our part creates larger issues with others.

We deal with numbers and money all day—all the time—in all we do. Accuracy is vitally important to not only us but to all those on the other side of the "coin". It is paramount in running a bank and balancing hundreds, if not thousands, of transactions on a daily basis. It takes a ton of effort and oversight and consciousness to keep every penny balanced and accounted for. We have redundant systems in place that help us to accomplish this task every day (With all that said, we do a great job!).

But beyond the computer and daily "right-on" balancing, it goes beyond every other little detail that we must be ever mindful of for our accuracy. Those being in our interactions with customers, in all forms of communications both written or verbal. Accuracy impacts and affects you, the customers, your coworkers, and many others we may never see or think about.

Being accurate is being a professional, and it is fundamental to our core value of building confidence.

"To make you know the certainty of the words of truth.
That you may correctly answer..."
—Proverbs 22:21

35

"Think tomorrow is today, and plan for it."

MY THOUGHTS EACH week are spurred by things that have happened, taken my attention or time, things that have moved me or caused me to ponder and were very relevant the week before. There have been a ton of different things over the years and the vast majority has been work related as that truly has most of my attention during the week. Even though this week was busy, and there could have been a work-related thought, something very close to my heart holding my attention. This thought takes some liberties, but as all my thoughts are being placed in a file for futures to have and read later this one was very important to me.

My attention and focus behind this week's thought is my daughter as she turned eighteen this past Friday. When she was born, I was right there and was elated when the Doc said, "You have a little girl." That was all I ever wanted. I had many thoughts racing through my mind this week, some being that day in detail, as it hit me those eighteen years have come and gone too quickly and now she has only a few months left in our home before she takes off to college. Sobering to say the least, as many of you have or will face this same thing, especially last week, seeing her walk in her last debutante ball. I thought back over those eighteen years and remembered all the good memories with her growing up, holding her early on, the three-to-four age when she was clinging to me, with me all the time. The first time she rode her bike by herself, the times she would ride with me on my motorcycle or horses, her first day of school, all the Gonzales What-a-burger breakfasts we shared every school morning, her cheerleader games, track meets, her graduation from SGISD eighth grade, buying her a promise ring, when she started to drive, the livestock shows, and her first date. There have been many wonderful memories and good things that have happened over the years.

Melyn has pictures in her room of her with my dad, grandfather, and a ton of friends over the eighteen years. On my desk is a picture of me with my uncle holding Melyn for the first time. This is important to me as it sets a priority for the responsibility I have with her. It reminds me of where I was and what I knew I had to do to provide, protect, and give her a future. I was thinking then of what she would become, where she would be, and what she would do in her life. I was thinking, tomorrow is today and we should plan for it. We planned and waited over seven years for her, as we had to get Kim through college, to her first teaching job, save enough down payment for our first house, and then save for the hospital and delivery cost. We did the best we could starting from scratch to have a home for her.

I now know how the first eighteen years with her mother and me turned out. I anticipate, with some excitement, what she will do with the rest of her life and who she'll become. My gift for her this year was a birthday card with a personal love note and a figurine of a father holding a new baby. I wanted her to know I was thinking of her on that day and will every day forward. A written note to be a physical reminder for her to see on her shelf every morning.

Every week, I think about what to write and it is funny what confirmation comes in some cases. As I was contemplating writing this one, it was more personal in nature, someone I had not met came up to me last evening at the bank party and told me that they read each of my thoughts and because of that, they felt they knew me because of those written words even though they'd never met me before that day. That is where the point of my personal thought ties back to us this week. We need to build true relationships (find a connection) with others—a bond, something that is sticky and holds them to us. As in this conversation, I was able to connect with someone I never met because of my weekly thoughts.

What we do every day really is that important. We impact lives, we can and do change other's futures, and we do those things whether we realize it or not. Our actions, intended or unintended, affect tomorrows and what others will do. So let's be ever mindful that the todays really do determine the tomorrows. Do your best to show your trueness, practice excellence in all things, make real, meaningful, and positive impacts on others, show outward appreciation and the value we all bring, add the stickiness that monetary things alone cannot bring. Show folks so they have no doubts that we are real people who care about their future.

Be out every day working hard, creating confidence and trust.

"Dwell in the land and cultivate faithfulness."

—Ps. 37:3

36

"Today is important, but tomorrow matters."

I WROTE THIS in one of the last paragraphs of my thought last week. I firmly believe this and have been trying to live it daily. To me, today and tomorrow are equally important, as you cannot have one without the other. Think about this: how would tomorrow look if you gave no thought to today? What would today look like if you gave absolutely no thought to tomorrow? How does thinking about the future affect what you do today and how tomorrow turns out? Think about that. Your todays determine, in many ways, your tomorrows.

Last year, I received a call from one of our customers asking me if I would visit with a young man. I told her I would and soon thereafter a young man was waiting to see me. Right off the bat. I could see there was something about this young man, clean cut, shake your hand, look you in the eye—overall focused. As we started to speak, I knew he had a "life" plan. He was starting college here and was looking for a place to stay, work, and, overall, some connections. He was very likable and I enjoyed talking to him. As we started to visit, it became very apparent this young man was a little different than most.

He was already involved with his county politics, working, as well as having his own small business. He had to make his own way. I asked him if he played sports in high school and he told me he did for a year but realized he would not play college ball or anything better, so he thought it wiser in the long run to focus on areas that would help him later in life. Now that is a forward thinker. He had a portfolio of references, a resume, and a personal introduction letter that was clear of where he was going. I asked him what he wanted to be and he told me the Governor of the State of Texas.

Here is a funny bit of our talk, but it tells you something about him. As we talked about his skills and what kind of work he wanted, we ran down his job history and skills. We were headed toward more agriculture-related work. He could see where it was going. To head that off, he told me, "I would not be opposed to working inside—like here in the bank." As he said this, he used his hand to wave about my office. He then clarified he didn't mean right in my office, but in the lobby. Now that is a young man who thinks and doesn't get himself into a hole. After the interview, I called our customer back and told her what a breath of fresh air the young man was. This kid had something most young people don't. He had a drive and he thought about tomorrow. By the way, this young man is currently heavily involved at TAMUK, people are starting to know him, and he is making his way around driving his King Ranch truck. He is now leading a city-wide merchant-promoting campaign that he presented to the Chamber of Commerce a couple of weeks back.

As I was thinking about what to write about, I really thought it relevant to drive home the point from last week. To further solidify that, I turned on my iPod and was listening to Marvin Gaye's "Too Busy Thinking About My Baby" on the way to the Bank. That song is on my iPod for one reason: Melyn. I played that song for her when she was born and for years afterward. Every time it comes on, I tell her it's her song from me to her. It is all about a man who has a one-track mind for his baby and he "ain't got time for nothing else". To me that song tells a story of what is important. If you are thinking about what is important and nothing else, where does that get you? I hope doing that gets you to what and where you want to be, if not, you may not be on the right track.

We all need to have drives in life that instill a fire in us to get us motivated, inspired, and moving forward. Those may be different and varied, but to me the best are internal. Some need a little outside fuel to really make them a reality in some cases. As an example, my personal drives were instilled (bred into me) early on. Those resulting drives are my two girls (my wife and daughter) at home who depend on me and lifelong goals that I had since I was very young. What are yours? Have you thought about those? Are you really serious? What are you doing today, right now, to make them a reality? How does Kleberg Bank fit in as "driver" and what are you doing to be a positive "driver" in Kleberg Bank for its success and for other staff? To me a driver connects to the core and it looks for the daily opportunities that life presents—and it does not waste them.

As we think about the whats, wheres, and big-picture tomorrows for the bank, our families and maybe even ourselves, we must always keep in mind, so do others. That is what makes our chosen careers in banking so important. As I say, "what we do is that important," we have the resources to help others' tomorrows really matter. Every person we come in contact with is important and their tomorrows are too. We need to take the time to really think about what makes a customer not only successful today but tomorrow and well beyond that.

Today is important but tomorrow matters. If we think about the future, we will do the right thing today. That ensures a successful tomorrow for all. Build foundations today that will last well into the future.

"Storing up for themselves the treasure of a good foundation for the future, so that they may take hold of that which is life indeed."
—1 Timothy 6:19

37

"A revelation is just that, it is having something clearly revealed (unhidden)."

A TRUE REVELATION is really finding out something hidden or unknown to you that is valuable and may be just the ticket you were looking for. The definition of revelation is: 1. The act of revealing or disclosing; disclosure, 2. Something revealed or disclosed, especially a striking disclosure, as of something not before realized, 3. Theology, something thus communicated or disclosed. Something that contains such disclosure as the Bible, 4. The last book in the New Testament; the Apocalypse. Have you ever had something revealed that was like "Man, that is so clear, I should have seen that before" or "Now I understand where this person is coming from, did that, or is thinking that way". That is really cool to be at that point where you can use that understanding to create better results than you could have ever expected as well as enable the other party to have their expectations exceeded.

This past week, I had two true "revelations" when talking to two different people about two totally different items. Both revealed to me something that brought me great value as I needed to have that information. It showed me reasons (in these cases) for the other person's causes for hesitations and concerns. In both cases where the concern or hesitation was revealed, it was something I really needed and wanted to understand what was the underlying core. To get those "revelations", I had to use two different approaches because both were different scenarios and the people were different. But the underlying factor was my desire to really find that "nugget".

One, I had to ask straight up after a prior conversation then wait for an open response. The other, I had to listen hard for those keywords and then put those with prior conversations to make it all connect. So, when I heard the first person and their underlying thoughts it was like a spotlight came on. I quickly understood the concerns and addressed those quickly. These will end up a win-win for both sides. The other revelation was a key in that person's thought process that I needed to understand. I can now address that as time goes forward. I think sometimes a revelation may get postponed, missed, or not totally received when either party may be slightly at fault.

One for not communicating clearly, not being or feeling 100 percent open, or holding back. The other for either not taking the effort to understand or not asking, "Help me understand that more and let me hear your thoughts or concerns." Listening, digging for more, and watching body language cues may all be required to get to the core revelations. But to me it starts with wanting to find the revelation (nuggets) and putting the effort out first. A better analogy is if you don't want to put together a puzzle then don't open the box and then surely don't dump the pieces on the table as the puzzle will not magically put itself together. All it will be is a bunch of pieces cluttering up a clean tabletop.

What is so important about a revelation and how does it affect us? First, if it is a revelation, it should bring something of value. That means, value to both parties not just one as that gets back to the ultimate win-win scenario and that is where the true treasure lies. Once you receive that vital information, you need to protect and then quickly act upon those in a manner that matches the environment which enables more revelations to come later. So, imagine you are talking to a customer and in that conversation something is revealed that is so clear your light bulb goes on. Then it is up to you 100 percent to act upon that message. Sometimes those nuggets are buried in the conversations, letters, emails, comments, maybe something unsaid that is easy to read, etc. It may not even be clear to the customers, but can be brought to life, if we take the initiative to dig in and ask all the right questions. Again, it starts with our efforts and wanting to get to the core. The question is really, what is the underlying issue (positive or negative)? That nugget may be a variety of solutions from the positive meeting to exceeding the customer's expectations, maybe even their dreams or bringing resolve to a concern. Maybe it puts to rest the doubts that may rise about the things to come or not to come in the future.

"That by revelation there was made known
to me the mystery."
—Eph. 3:3

38

"Silence is really not golden – it can actually rob you and others of the gold."

WE HAVE ALL heard the old adage, "silence is golden." Now I am in agreement that listening is a great virtue and you learn a lot from hearing what others have to say. A big part of our job is to listen to the needs of others. But, having said that, not saying anything when the signals are loud and clear can and will kill the chance of us making payroll. Twice in the last week, "the sound of dead air" stopped or stagnated a sale that I needed. I was in need of a hay ring for round bales. I had seen what I was looking for at a local store, so I stopped by to look at their lot. I went into the store and inquired about it. I was told it was sold. By the way, it had sat out there from the time the store opened, I was told.

When I asked what the price was, they had to look it up on the computer. I then asked about another hay ring and its price. I asked if any were in stock, but neither model was on hand. So, I had to ask when they would get more in and the response was they did not know. There was a manager standing there listening to the whole conversation, and he did not say anything either. With no response or suggestion they could order it for me, I walked out of the store, nothing in hand and they had no sale.

While driving through Robstown a few days later, I stopped by a well-known store and saw they had a large stack of hay rings in the parking lot. I went in the store and picked up a sack of feed and asked about the hay ring and prices. The clerk had a large earring in his ear, a rock style T-shirt and a cap cocked to the side. He checked me out, and I went outside toward the stack of hay rings. While waiting, two of the staff walked out to their cars and saw me out of the corner of their eyes. Neither of them asked to help me as they drove out of the parking lot. So, I got the opportunity to walk back into the store to find out where the summoned staff member was. As I waited, I saw one staff member reloading the coke box and pitching a coke to another staff worker.

Finally, the clerk asked me, and I told him I was still waiting. He called, and the one that was pitched the coke shuffled to the back to get keys and shuffled his feet out to the parking lot toward the hay racks. He saw that he needed tin snips to cut the metal binding on the racks. While he shuffled slowly back to the store, I found a separate stack of hay rings with no binding on them. I called out to him a few times before he shuffled back to the racks and started to unlock the chain that linked all the equipment together. He and another staff member with no uniform loaded the hay ring, then I had to ask for a tie down. Of which he started to shuffle back to the store to get some rope. I decided in the essence of time to do it myself and got some rope out of my toolbox to tie it down before he got back. So, after that you might think a small thank you for shopping with us or thanks for buying the equipment might work, but I believe that was too much effort on both as they just stood there then walked off. I know, by reading these two little stories, you can tell that I was not in the least irritated or put-out.

Here is the lesson, we must not make our customers do our jobs. We should not make the customer have to ask or tell us what we need to do. Both of the cases were me driving the transaction. Think how much easier it would have been if the stores would have driven the transaction by asking my needs, offering the right product, and then closing the deal. They would have made money, I would have gotten what I needed, and both would have saved tons of time. Although, I would have been without a "thought for the week". So, what they did caused one store to totally miss a sale and the other to waste a lot of time and give poor service. I think there are a ton of lessons of "do nots" in these two examples. We need to not be the talk of these types of transactions but be the talk of extraordinary service and professionalism. We need to be the first responders and the problem solvers. Staying with the customer all the way to the end and making sure the customers got what they needed in a service better than expected. Exceeding expectations can only happen when we actually do that very thing. I wonder how many deals are lost each day in the business world as silence robs many of the gold? Do not make the customer have to work, that is our job and that is what they pay us for. What happens everyday as a result of our contact with customers makes payroll.

"...for the laborer is worthy of his wages."
—Luke 10:7

A little extra that a friend of mine from NYC sent to me to go along with this thought:

Chad,

Really enjoyed "Silence is not Golden"". I have attached a story that I always use when teaching leadership—it is called, ""Remember me?"". Runs parallel to your Thought.

Enjoy. God bless.

REMEMBER ME?

Remember me? I'm the fellow who goes to a restaurant, sits down, and waits patiently while the waitresses do everything BUT take my order.

I'm the fellow who goes into a department store and stands quietly while the sales clerks finish their chit-chat.

I'm the one who goes to a gas station and never blows his horn, but waits patiently while the attendant finishes reading his comic book.

You might say that I'm a good guy, but you know who else I am?

I'm the fellow who never comes back! And it amuses me to see you spend thousands of dollars every year to get me back when I was there in the first place.

All you had to do, to keep me, was give me a little service and show me a little courtesy. Remember me?

39

"There will be opportunities you never would have dreamed would happen in your life."

I HAVE SAID in the past that "All things happen for a reason for those that believe". Kim tells Melyn to not doubt, things can happen, and you never know what will. We've had some really cool "Forrest Gump" moments in our life and Melyn has been there to see a few firsthand.

As I start to write this one, my mind wanders back to the training I received when I first got into banking. I thought about the influences that impressed me early in life, little things that were imbedded in my psyche, becoming a part of my drive. Those little life magnets that are started way back. pulling you toward your destined life. I thought about that at the time and knew that was true because even at twenty-three or twenty-four, I was already acting like those folks I was patterning after, even with the worldly things I was pursuing.

So, I say all this to come to my point. What you do and where you end up are internally self-generated in a large part. They are then added to when those really cool life experiences come along. Those life gifts that you have to make a conscious decision to take and do so with commitment and sacrifice. Last weekend was one of those times. I had a conflict for that date and went with my earlier commitment to this event.

As I walked over to the tables that were loaded with what I would have never dreamed I would have been able to see firsthand, handled, and then fired. National Treasure firearms had me excited. There were the guns of my childhood and even through today. The ones I grew up watching and still do every Saturday. There it was to me the holy grail of western guns the real Chuck Connor's "The Rifleman" rifle with the lever screw to make it fire every time you brought the lever back up. Along with that were several John Wayne Colt single action revolvers and big loop Winchester '92 rifles (yep, the Big Jake one was there). And not to leave out Clint Eastwood's Outlaw Josey Wales Walkers and Dirty Harry's .44 Magnum.

That weekend was full from early morning to late in the evening on both days and the reason my writings were postponed to this next week was to give me time to really grasp and share the deeper experience. It was not only the once in a lifetime opportunity to see and handle the firearms, but I was also one of the very few on the firing line who was given the responsibility to load and handle each of these guns for the other participants. The gift to meet some really cool folks I hope very soon to see again was another bonus. I wondered how in the world I got to that day and even to the organization I joined. When I was growing up, I never would have dreamed of doing so.

I was watching a western true mini-series this weekend and one of the lines in the movie was, "What do you want out of this life?" The other person says, "Just to get through it." I thought what a sad line and outlook. Life presents gifts and opportunities every day—some are very obvious with huge wrappings and bows on them and others are those pearls in a shell that you have to go digging for. Either way they take someone with a good eye and the heart to go after them.

Every day we have the life gift to change someone's day and present to them opportunities. Opportunities others may or may not present to them. That is what makes us unique—that little extra effort to go beyond and do better for others. I thought of the owner of the firearms. What if he had just said, "You know, these are treasures, and I don't want to risk those out? I'll just hold them locked up and not share those with folks." He could have thought, "I really don't want to drive from California to Texas on my own dime to donate all my time, efforts, and assets to help an organization." What if? That weekend would have never happened.

You see, we all have to do our part to ensure that other's dreams and needs are met. Life is not to do on your own and everybody needs somebody. This world is an interactive puzzle. We all hold a piece, and if we don't put in our pieces, we hold those out, somebody's full life experience may (including our own) not come to pass or be incomplete.

Do your best this week to do your part and help someone say, "I would have never dreamed that would happen."

"As each has received a gift,
use it to serve one another."
—1 Peter 4:10

40

“Rain may stop some while others will find opportunities to get other things done.”

ALL THE RAIN has kept farmers from harvesting crops and working outside jobs. When rain comes to those who depend on good weather to work outdoors, it gives only options to catch up elsewhere. When you need to run a combine on dry crops and you have rain pouring down there is not much you can do. Or if you need to construct a home that needs dry conditions so materials are not exposed to the elements, you face a no-go as well. Even though those that rely on good weather to work may not be able to do their primary job those that see the opportunity to find other work can stay ahead overall. Think about most construction and agriculture jobs. All rely on equipment and all have to do some paperwork and or bookkeeping. Would you suspect those that are in their shops doing repair or maintenance work on their equipment would be using their time wisely? Or taking that time to review where they are on current billings and possible tax work. Both maintenance and current book work are vital to running these types of business for, if not, you will have breakdowns and financial issues. Taking that opportunity to maintain and catch up when rain comes may actually not be all that bad. Rain is needed to refuel the soil, and time is needed to do other things. I think about those who sit around during these times as if they didn't have anything in their shop to catch up on. Are their finances up to date?

How do we react when rain (interruptions or distractions) comes to us? Do we take rain as an opportunity to sit and visit about it or do we find opportunities to catch up on—something else we are behind on. Or better yet, do we find new things that we have neglected to do? Rain to us may come in all forms. It may be one of many things that can provide interruptions during the day. Some interruptions may present opportunities to make money return later and others certainly will not. Some interruptions may be just a short rain shower and others a hurricane. But we must know that all interruptions need and require us to react. We either react towards or give in to the interruptions or we can focus on what the interruption brings to the bottom line. I think it deals with prioritizing your day and sticking with a focus to generate results. There are many distractions during the day. The main issue is how and what do we focus on and do we manage our time well? Are we looking for any little reason that comes along to give us an opportunity to delay what needs to get done? Do we chase a few rabbits that end up in nothing on the table at the end of the day? Do we cause others to get off track? Are we the rain? Do we spend time doing things that will not bring the results we need? When it does rain, do we need others to come tell us that there are shop and bookkeeping needs to accomplish or can we see the opportunity to do that on our own? If so, why do we need others to tell us to stay on point or ask us why something is not completed?

It is going to rain now and then and disruptions will come every day that will distract us. It will be up to us to take a distraction and make it an opportunity. It is up to us alone to not procrastinate more and give in to those rain showers. Rain delays are not always bad as they give us a chance to catch up. In our world there have been many national rain showers and some global financial hurricanes and while others say “I cannot”, “we used to do that”, “I just wait until it stops raining”, we need to look for all those new opportunities. While the others may be sitting around in a coffee shop, which we hope all our competitors are doing, we need to be looking for those new opportunities. So, when it does rain, and it will, we need to still keep working so when the rain stops we don't miss a beat and all the "equipment" and "books" are in good condition. Most of all, let's not add rain to someone else's day and cause them to have to stop their focus and production. We all need to assist each other in staying on track and, when possible, give a hand to those who may have a little more. We are all accountable for our time.

"...for the laborer is worthy of his wages."

—Luke 10:7

41

"Always remember a door swings both ways."

ONE SHOULD ALWAYS remember, a door both opens and closes. It can also be locked or blocked by many things. I think, in life, we should think about these doors as opportunities that present themselves each day. Each opportunity is like a door, and it opens up to something new and possibly life changing. Every day, we will have things presented to us that will open up doors or close them, and we never want to be in situations where one is locked or we do things that add blocks. Opportunities, like any real doors must be passed through, but you have to know where the doors are and sometimes how to open those doors. You have to know where to go to get in and have those keys (skills, passions, and drive) to get in. Just like in every workday, we have to know where we are going and what our goals are. Focused on the tasks at hand. You cannot just wander around aimlessly hoping someone will take you by the hand and lead you to your desk. Be alert, know doors are out there and be ready to open them up and take every bit of what those doors offer you.

One should remember that doors are meant to be used by more than one person. They were not made to be used by only one person. Can you imagine if every building had to have individual doors for everyone that used that building? If doors could not be shared or used by others it would create some issues. A building could face severe structural issues and may even fall down, there would be no support walls. One thing to remember is, when someone does open a door, you should be ready to give others that same opportunity. Doors that have been opened to me, I have tried to open for others. It has made that opportunity even better.

Just this past weekend, I was able to open a door for others with an opportunity that had been offered to me years ago. This is going to make that opportunity (door) even bigger and better for all those who opened that door for me. I think this is where many good things come and those opportunities even get larger. Keeping the doors open for the ones who have those character traits needed to grow that opportunity. Many folks have built greater opportunities and added the next level when giving others the keys to doors that they would never have walked through themselves. It is really about building strong relationships and building those networks of like-minded passion-driven folks. That makes life great.

What is sad are all those doors left unopened to those first folks who never will get to offer to others. When this happens many numbers of people lose out. Don't miss opportunities for yourself that you can share and build with others. Be alert and make that extra effort to open doors. I often see those who simply walk by a door, some doors that are even open, and they either do not see it or do not want to do what it takes to walk through. Let's not be those. Let's be those who take advantage of every opportunity presented to us daily. So we all win and build an even greater bank for all those to come behind us.

Every day, we should see ourselves as doorkeepers and we must be willing to open doors of opportunities and be ready to share with those who can add to and build upon the opportunities to make them even bigger and better than when they were offered to us.

"To him the doorkeeper opens..."

—John 10:3

42

"A positive frame of mind (outlook) creates opportunities."

THIS HIT ME as a "revived" revelation this past Friday. It is something I always knew, but it just seemed to all come together and fit then. It is an accumulation of recent reads, a video, years of watching and studying folks, and current reflections. All that hit me with the above thought: a positive frame of mind (outlook) creates opportunities, and further, it even affects who we are and what may eventually come about. It is mainly mental.

This past week, I was focused on work with no time for other thoughts. Friday evening, a farrier came out to the house to trim the horses. We always have a good visit and time (keyword) to enjoy. I always look forward to seeing Steve. As he was packing up to leave, my blue heeler came over, and it reminded him of a video saved on his phone. The video really tied into all the other thoughts and reads I had recently. The video was about a farrier that was given a dog that became his ticket to new life opportunities and experiences (nationwide as well as the internet) he would have never had. He and his dog, Skidboot, have made all the major TV talk shows, won dog competitions, and he has spoken at all types of events and venues. What made the video even better, I think, was the owner's outlook on life. His underlying message on life, as well as his interaction with the dog, transcended a great influence on the audiences and made the amazing things this dog could do even more unique.

As I thought back on others who have influenced me and made a positive difference in general, it has been their mental drive that has stuck with me. That is what hit me. It is their "frame of mind"—that internal something that allows them to function in a way that others may not or possibly cannot do. And even though the cross section of people I am thinking of may have different personalities, different ages, and different career fields, they all have this one thing in common. It separates them and holds them apart from others. This does not come easy, and it takes a conscious decision to keep mentally in check, to stay resilient and focused.

To us this week, everyone can and does change the outcome of a personal interaction, either good or bad, it may all depend on their "frame of mind". We see it every time we shop or have services provided by others, we come away thinking about how good or not good the experience was. Think, have you ever had a bad experience that was either started or enhanced by another's "frame of mind"? You walk away thinking, "What in the world are you doing, do you really care, what is the deal?" Could that have been better if their outlook was different? We all know the answer to that one and how that changed our day. I think, how one gets up and how one anticipates the day in part sets the tone, but it goes deeper and is driven by the "frame of mind". It starts with a daily commitment, if one gets up thinking nothing is going to happen, it is going to be a dull day, or this day is going to be bad, I can guarantee that you have just set the tone and mentally you are already there. Think the opposite, you get up with a positive mindset that "today is the day that I can and will make a difference and things are going to happen today—no doubts—I am going to be a part of things." The challenges come during the day when you must decide not to allow derailments, no matter what the size, or any other things change your initial frame of mind, and I am focused and strong no matter what other folks do or say to try to change that.

You have to remain in control.

We need to be the changers and influencers that set a positive, excellent, Take-Care-of-Business, confidence-building, character-based experience. We need to set the tone of what happens and how that makes one's life better. It all starts with an internal decision.

Opportunities are presented daily, so we need the right frame of mind to set the tone, make the decision, and then act on it.

"Being of the same mind … intent on one purpose."
—Phil. 2:2

43

"Roadblocks can create new pathways."

LAST WEEK, WHILE in Austin to see Melyn for one of the last baseball games, this thought crossed my mind as we drove through traffic. We all know what detours, road delays, and dead-stop traffic can do. It can drive you crazy and throw off all that you need to be doing. It can affect more than time, it can affect your mental attitude and really what the outcome will be going forward.

So, as I drove through the heavy traffic, for whatever reason, I thought of how my mom started off young with her first job in Austin. And years later, Melyn did the same. On her own, new town, new place to live, new job, and new people all around her. Then, I thought back to how that Austin job and those detours and new pathways got Mom to where she is and that ultimately got me, in part, to where I am today. When you really think about it, we are all where we are in a large part today because of decisions made by those before us. Some of us might not be here today, if different life choices would have been made back then. In my case, looking back at my family and myself, it has been the job opportunities that drove and created life-directing changes.

Thinking more on the traffic analogy, even in heavy traffic or detours you just can't go with the flow and hope all will work out. You need to do your part to think ahead and look for what options there are. A few months back, I was in a dead stop (miles backed up) highway traffic. When I finally got to a high point in the road, I grabbed my binoculars out of the console and looked ahead to see what in the world was the deal and what options I had to get going again. You can't miss the exit ramp or be so far over that you can't get off when the opportunity comes. If you do that, you are in the hold of the others and you will miss where you want to end up or, if you do get there, you will miss your time.

To validate this point and to further a life example, I was watching the anniversary special on "The Beach Boys" this weekend. As they interviewed the group, minus the two Wilson brothers that have now passed on (one to cancer and the other to a diving accident), it was very interesting to see how all the originals are all back together today. One of those singers was the young neighbor boy who lived across the street from the three Wilsons. He was on the first five albums and toured with them until a conflict with Maury Wilson (the dad) ran him off. Timing is everything and here it is, all those years later, and he is now back center stage to take his rightful spot. So, sometimes a road block can be temporary, and if you stay on track and keep your wits, it can bring you right back to your direction, no matter what or who may be in your way.

We impact others every day!

It may be just a simple smile and greeting that makes someone feel special and important. It may be the only positive contact they have all day, so it is that important to someone else that we always do our absolute best to communicate and interact with them. We also need to not be roadblocks or detours to others as what we do impacts and affects not only the person we are talking to but their families, employees, and many others.

We need to always do our best to look for options that offer the best solutions to help others get to where they need and want to be. Looking down the road and not just at the bumper in front of you, is a good thing to do once in a while. It not only helps you make the right life decision today but everyone else who gets impacted by our personal decisions, actions, directives, and influences down the road.

"...be wise and direct your heart in the way."
—Proverbs 23:19

44

"You are kind, you are smart – you are important."

THIS IS A quote from the movie "The Help". This movie came out in 2011, and my wife, being a literature major and having read the book, could not wait to see it. So we did, and I have to admit for a "chick flick", it was a pretty good movie. It had some really solid, underlying messages and moral undertones. This quote was spoken to a young girl by her caregiver who, to say the least, did not have to say those words. Every day, this was spoken to the young girl—you are kind, you are smart, you are important. Think, as a young person, someone looking you in the eyes, saying those words in a heartfelt way while they were holding, how would that make you feel? Do you think you might believe and act on those words today and later in life as well?

What made me think about this movie line were several things spoken and heard over the past two weeks. One was a song I heard for the first time and the other were messages from two different people. All had the same underlying tone and dealt with: WORDS. The focus points of each may be a little different as one message dealt more with dreams and life goals and not letting others dampen those. That message had the same underlying message as the movie quote, with the question posed, "What if you heard a positive life-asserting message? What if you heard the exact opposite?" Examples were given of both and the point was: usually, what you heard was what you turned out to be. The second message was on influence. It centered on, should you or do you allow others to influence and control you? It dealt with not letting others steal your joy or dampen your spirits. In other words, do not let others control you emotionally.

The song "Words" matched these above as a refrain goes: "Words can build us up. Words can break us down. Start a fire in our hearts, or put it out." What was funny was that someone came up to me this past week and asked if I'd heard the message, sharing their thoughts on it. These two messages probably hit home with more than a few folks. As an example of this, a young man came to my office this past week to ask for my advice on a personal long-range matter. This was a big goal, and he is ready, dreaming big, and looking for a way to make it happen all on his own. I told him that I see and understand his motivation and drive, and gave him some thoughts on accomplishing this huge goal. I made it clear that getting help and looking for partners is not a bad thing and it leverages this plus many other things to come. Before he left, I told him I have no doubts he is going to be successful, I've seen what he is doing now and he has what it takes. He just needs the right folks to guide him and invest in him.

We all need help in life. Absolutely no one is perfect and there will never ever be. Yes, the old saying "no one is an island" is true to the core. We all need others to get us to where we are going and want to be. There is no one that can ever get to where they want on their own, as there are way too many pieces in anything life offers. When others come to you and express where they are headed and you can walk with them, do it. I can guarantee you it will be just as rewarding as when others stepped up to help you get to where you are or where you may want to ge.

Let's think about how and what we say to everyone and then watch the results. Watching the aftermath of those spoken words influence others every day. We do that in our words spoken and in our actions. What we do really is that important and it makes us—yes, it does—important. We need to take the lead on setting the stage in all we do or say. Think about this, what if you controlled the first words or set the tone in any interaction? If it was positive, do you think it would swing the outcome? What if it started off negative? Do you think that would swing the outcome? When we speak, let's think about the movie quote and decide we are kind, we are smart, and, yes, we are important. All these things act like positive life-changing agents for others.

"Therefore encourage one another and build up one another, just as you also are doing."
—Thess. 5:11

45

"An encouraging, affirming note goes a long way."

I HAVE ALWAYS written notes to Melyn ever since she was little. They may be a letter or just a note stuck in her school stuff to be found and read later. Recently, they have transitioned into texts and some of those are just a quick "luv ya". But I also want to send her something reassuring from her daddy. What made me think of this thought this week were those notes to her. There is something very important that I have always told her in my notes as well as verbally that was confirmed in a note sent by another. Recently, Melyn's picture was in the local paper and that clipping was mailed to her along with a note from something we are a part of. In that note were the same exact words that I have been telling her since I started to write her notes. It was confirming to her what I always spoke to her. Written notes (words) are that important.

I think we can all recall or we maybe even have saved notes from those who brought something of lasting value. I have framed handwritten notes and a picture of my uncle and me in my bedroom. The words in those notes from him are still speaking to me because they're specific words, to say the least, holding prophetically, goals in life. To further solidify my thought, I was digging among some papers this weekend, trying to find a car title, and in doing so, I found a stack of letters I have saved. Those letters are all handwritten from folks I respect who took time to know me well enough to write words that were meaningful and encouraging, building me up enough to save years later. I stopped writing this thought to pick one of those letters out to read again. After reading that letter it was just like the first time I got it and just as powerfully connecting. I think that words last long after someone or even seasons of life pass on and those written words in someone's own hand is like a treasure as it is a part of them that carries on. Think on this, can you still hear someone speak to you and hear the tone and their actual voice? Words are that powerful and directing.

To us this week, thinking again of what we do and say (verbal and written). We have very important roles in the lives of folks who depend on us for financial services and even beyond that. There has always been something very special to me when others say, "That is my bank" or "He/She is my banker". That to me is a lot to live up to as those words hold trust, confidence, safekeeping, security, and responsibility, to name a few. I think words again are that important and can be reassuring. I was speaking to someone this week about a customer's conversation and those words, "need to be reassuring", were used. That is significant because we all need to be reassured at times. Words, especially written ones, can bring that security and even build trust. Take the time to write handwritten notes to assure others of their value, maybe even their place in life, something connecting, something that builds them up, reassures character strengths and always, always something that shows without a doubt appreciation and thankfulness.

"Do not let kindness and truth leave you …
write them on a tablet."
—Proverbs 3:3

46

"We build something every day."

WE BUILD SOMETHING everyday whether we know it or not. We help others build and finance all sorts of things and, most importantly, we build relationships. Over my years of banking, I have had the opportunity to build and finance a bunch of different things, create relationships, and learn a lot along the way. It has always been a drive and encouragement to be a part of building something. Building something that I knew would last and be a part of the future. Building and moving forward and not just being status quo or stagnant but increasing for a greater plan. I can think back on those projects and remember being there with others for the opening of doors, the expansions, the new equipment running and ribbon cuttings. It was pretty cool knowing that the bank and all those there had a part in making those dreams come to a reality. Those dreams create; they create economic benefits and opportunities for many. They build commerce as well as all those family homes built along the way.

This thought was very clear to me as I walked into a beautiful new hotel we financed. As I walked through the doors, the first thing I saw was the newness of it all, the rush of anticipation from the customers. The reservations were already being taken. I watched the hotel staff rushing around, putting on the final touches and checking all the details. Everyone was on final lookout and ready to go. There was even a management consultant from Midtown, New York City, checking it all out as this was a major company's first hotel in South Texas. As I walked around the project and visited with the owners, managers, speaking to the employees, I could see and feel the excitement. This was a really big deal, and I felt, as I sat with the owners, and knew we all had a part in this and helped provide resources to make this happen. As I felt that come over me, I told them with all sincerity, "Thank you for allowing us the opportunity to have a part in this project." The "Financed by Kleberg Bank" sign had been on site from the start of construction and many folks saw that and knew we really do build things. We all helped build a new project that will be here for years and that will create a place of rest and relaxation for many that come to South Texas. We had a part in providing jobs to many who take those paychecks and provide for families. This is exactly why I always say, "What we do really is that important." We build things everyday.

This week, we have so many opportunities, many right under our noses and all around us. Let's not miss those. Always look around and keep your eyes open for every little opportunity to build—build each other up, build the bank, and build our communities. Do not let one day slip by when we lose an opportunity to build. Focus on building up and not tearing down. When we wake up, we should make a decision to create and build as that is first and foremost. It has to be made before we move forward. To me, building has a critical factor and that is the underlying relationships. Again, this is where we put the rebar and steel in the slabs. We need to build relationships on the core values of this bank everyday. Build relationships with our customers that leave no doubts with them. Relationships built on character, trust, and complete confidence are relationships we can rely on.

Do your absolute best every day and practice DTR (Done Today Right). We need excellence in all that we do and say. Build with pride every day.

"...a time to build up."

—Ecc. 3:3

47

"Take care with your work and keep others in mind."

A FEW WEEKS back, when we were in a hotel, we pulled our clothes out of the suitcase and, to say the least, they were wrinkled. It is one of my "pet peeves" in life to have a shirt not properly pressed. Or worse, putting a shirt on, tying my tie, and reaching up to find a button cracked or missing. That right there will make me speak "French" early in the morning. For years I ironed my own shirts and could never get them to "cleaners" quality, so when I finally could afford it that was one of the first things I did. My shirts were starched and ironed at the cleaners. Again, I had an expectation for years of seeing what cleaner-quality shirts looked like. I expected them to be done right. Really think about this, if I or anyone else wanted less than professional quality, why not save the money, just do it yourself and save the aggravation. One of the things professional cleaners can do is roll your cuffs. They have a machine that can make the cuffs on your shirts round, not just pressed flat. When the cleaners changed hands they quit doing that and I had to ask over and over again for that service and the new owners would not do it. They always had an excuse. The quality dropped and then the shirts were going back. This went on for a while. Kim can still remember the day going in to pick up my clothes and they could not find them. Finally, one of the clerks said, "Oh, Mr. Stary's shirts are on the rack with…" It was two other customers who were as particular as me. These shirts all had a second review. But the question was why? Why not just do it right the first time and not have to do it again and again, dealing with inferior work and customer complaints and "bad press in the community"? What finally happened was a new cleaner came to town.

As we were getting ready to leave the hotel, Kim asked me to iron her blouse. As I did that (don't get the wrong picture as I do not normally do this) it hit me that this was her shirt she was about to wear out and I needed to do a careful job. As I ironed the creases and turned the shirt, I thought about that "care" factor and who I was doing this for. It made me think about today's thought. That is, when we are working, we need to think about the person we are providing the service for and take due care with it.

I really think if we would just think of that other person and add that level of concern, respect, and consideration, striving for the excellence factor, we would change the way we do things. I did that when I was ironing her shirt. I could have been half-hearted and done a quick press, but it struck me hard when I was ironing, that it was not about me wanting to iron that blouse, it was Kim asking me to help her as we were a little pressed for time and she deserved me doing it right. She has done a ton of my shirts right. So, why would she deserve anything but my best and my ultimate care? Why would we not do the same to our customers? Because we always need to stop and think about where and how we make our paychecks from time to time.

My point this week is, do we really think about others we are working for? When you are talking to a customer, taking a request, preparing the paperwork and all the other pieces, do you stop and think about that person? Do you think, "I am providing the same level of care that I would for someone I truly care about?" If not, you need to add that level of care. We need to put "care" into everything we do. If we do, it will show up in the process and in the final product. Folks, excellent service is not a trick or magic. It is about the basics: care, consideration, respect for others, having pride in your work, thinking of the one requiring the service (their time, their money, and their vision), being skilled about our jobs, and just working hard to have the above-expected, final results.

It all starts with a passionate commitment from each of us. We cannot have a slack day. That's the day that counts and that may be the day that we either gain or lose a customer. No slack days. Every day, we must be "in the game" when we walk through the door. We can't do anything less. We must come in, fired up and getting others motivated, spreading that excitement and providing that level of care that everyone who calls, walks in, or hits our internet site deserves.

"That there should be no division in the body, but that the members should have the same care for one another."
—1 Cor. 12:25

48

"You have it, so never let anyone tell you differently and stifle your passion or talents."

I WAS AT an IBAT bank conference last week and walked through the service entrance to come around to the back of the ballroom where a meeting was going on. As I walked down the hallway, I could not help but notice a man who was bending down to pick up some bags. He had a different look than what I was expecting from a worker in the hotel. I went in and heard the first speaker. After that the CEO of IBAT came up to introduce the next speaker. It was the man I saw in the hallway.

He was our guest speaker from California, an artist who specializes in leadership, strategic/excellence, and embracing change training. To say the least, this guy was good because he used his given talents to share and pour into others.

He began his talk about the left brain/right brain background and how creative we all are at a young age and how that declines over the years. He asked how many can draw and, of course, no hands were raised. He asks that same question when he goes to high schools and then to elementary schools. The results: in high school, about 10 percent raise their hands, and at elementary schools, 100 percent do. Why do you think that is, and what changes as we get older? One thing the speaker brought out that really stuck with me and I think we all have examples of this is what others speak to us that limit or stifle us. The critical factor in life. The speaker told of when this changed for him in the fourth grade. He was coloring in class one day, outside the lines, and a teacher gave him very negative comments of how he could not draw or color. That critical speaking had him not creating any art from that time until very later in life. The chance to pick up a brush came after a life change where he lost everything after 9/11 when the financial markets took a hit.

He went into the garage and started to paint and travels the world today, using his talents to teach. It is amazing how one person's harsh criticism stifled a man for years. What would have happened if that teacher would have been an encouragement? How many people would have never been motivated to stretch and go forward had he not had a life-changing event that got him back on the art path of his given talent and passions?

As he further spoke, he picked up a small nerf football and threw it into the larger crowd and hit a person whom I worked with at Wells Fargo years ago. He went out in the crowd and talked to him about challenging the fear factor. He gave him a choice to throw the football or come up on stage and do whatever the envelope said, which he was holding. The audience member decided to throw the football. The ball came across the huge ballroom and hit me square in the heart. So, I got called up in front of all the hundreds of bankers to answer a "fear factor" challenge. The challenge was to take the artwork he had just painted as a gift, a hand-painted picture of the Statue of Liberty. Afterwards, Kim came up, and I introduced him to her and told him that Kim taught history at the King Ranch high school. They began a conversation, and he gave her a training package that included a DVD. Now, she can take that same motivating message and pass it on to many young people for years. The multiplication of positive influence, now that is truly something. We have a choice every day for what we say and do, and we must always remember that it will, without a doubt, have a negative or positive impact. Let's find those internal talents and passions and use those to the very best of our abilities, once we do this, excellence will elude. These have to be self-generated and motivated as they come from within.

"Make every effort to confirm your calling and election.
For if you do these things, you will never stumble."
—2 Peter 1:9-11

About the Author

CHAD D. STARY is a career banker with over 37 years in the industry. His years of banking and business experiences in different Texas markets along with his family's instilled values and being reared in the small Texas town of Edna influenced these thoughts. Always passionate in his work and outside interests, he serves as the President and CEO of First State Bank of Uvalde and was the past Chairman of the Former Texas Rangers Foundation. He has been married to his loving and supportive wife of 34 years, Kim. They have one daughter Melyn Kate who is married to Jacob Yaklin.

Dedication

I dedicate this book to Mother Earth, who is in desperate need of healing. I also dedicate this book to you and to all human beings; we are the only ones that can heal this planet, and we must start by first healing ourselves. Lastly, I would like to dedicate this book to my loving parents. Without them I would not be able to share this message with you. Thank you all for all that you do, and thank you for taking the time to read this book, and for doing what it takes to heal the state of our world. Together we can create a better world for many generations to come.

Contents

Introduction

As you read these words, billions of living beings are suffering. Billions of people are living in poverty, starving from a lack of food, with no clean water to drink, and no way of maintaining their health, or of living a truly happy and fulfilling life.

Billions of animals are being tortured and abused in slaughterhouses, living their short lives in constant pain and fear, all so that humans can continue to use them for pleasure and profit.

Billions of trees are cut down every year, destroying the ecosystems that depend on them, and depleting the oxygen that we breathe, just so we can harvest their wood and use the land where they once stood, when there are plenty of other more sustainable options available.

Billions of people are suffering emotionally, unable to cope with their treatment from an entire society of people lacking in love and genuine compassion for one another.

War, famine, pollution, destruction, violence, oppression, racial injustice, torture, murder, genocide, deception, slavery—how can humanity allow such terrible things to happen? How can we be aware of the suffering that is happening on this planet, and not do anything at all to try to change it?

Are we really so comfortable in our ignorance that we choose to look away from these horrors purely for the sake of comfort, as if an entire planet full of suffering will somehow not affect us? As if we are not just as responsible for humanity's actions as anyone else? Are we really so preoccupied with our own lives that we can't even acknowledge what we are doing to the Earth?

The fact that humanity has allowed so much disaster to happen shows clearly our level of insanity. We have a delusional perception of life that causes us to behave in destructive and irrational ways. We are ignorant to the laws of nature and of our own existence, reflecting our mental confusion in every action that we take.

It is not our fault for thinking the way that we do; we merely adopted our ignorance from the generations of ignorant people before us, conditioned to be ignorant from the moment we were born. We are not to blame for our ignorance, but we are still responsible for our actions, and our delusional perception of life has produced far too much suffering.

Ignorance can no longer continue. We cannot turn our heads away from what is happening in the world and expect it to solve our problems. We need to change our way of life and how we interact with our environment, and this can only be done by first changing our way of thinking.

Every action is preceded by a thought. The way that we think and perceive greatly determines the way that we act and behave. If we want to change the way we treat the world, we have to change the way that we view the world, and especially the way we view ourselves in the world.

This change is necessary, and every human being who has been conditioned by society needs to evolve their ignorant perception of life, and become aware of the ways in which they impact the world.

This change is necessary, but it cannot be forced upon you. No one can make you change or force you to see

things from a new perspective. You have to be willing to see things differently than how you have been taught to see them. You have to be willing to accept that what you once thought to be true is actually false. You have to be willing to admit to your ignorance, let go of your conditioned beliefs, and begin replacing your ignorance with knowledge.

Ignorance can only be cured with knowledge, and in this book lies the knowledge to cure you of your ignorance and undo the conditioning that has formed your behavior—but if you do not have the desire to change, or do not have an open mind toward new information, the words in this book will be meaningless to you.

As much as humanity needs you to make this change, you can only change if you are willing to. These words are only able to convey a fraction of what is happening on the planet right now, but there are literally billions, if not trillions of living beings suffering from the results of our actions.

It may not seem like it, but we contribute to this suffering simply by remaining ignorant and submitting to the standards of an ignorant society. We all need to change our way of life and evolve past thousands of years of human ignorance. This might not be an easy task, and it may not be a task you thought you would ever have to perform, but we are at a crossroads between peace on Earth and self-destruction, and unless we want to destroy ourselves and countless other living beings, we have to move beyond our ignorance and adapt to a more loving, peaceful, and sustainable way of life.

We can make this transition from destroying the environment to healing the environment and realizing that we are not separate from the environment, but we have to be willing to change our current level of understanding, along with the disharmonic lifestyle that follows.

Naturally, we tend to move towards comfort, but the life we are comfortable with now is not in harmony with

Nature's laws. To change our way of living, we need to change our way of thinking, and shift our perspective to one that is in harmony with the way the Universe functions, no matter how uncomfortable this transition may make us feel at the time.

No one can force us to change. The blame is not on the governments, banks, corporations, media, and people that govern societies' laws. The blame is on us, the citizens, the people, the human beings that make up society and follow these laws made by man, rather than the laws of Nature.

We have to be willing to leave behind a way of thinking that no longer serves us, so we can embrace a new reality. We have to be open to new information, even if this information contradicts everything we once believed to be the truth. We have to be willing to face the truth, rather than hiding comfortably in our ignorance.

This book is a tool to aid you in the process of transformation, to provide you with the knowledge and understanding that is necessary for undoing your conditioning and healing the planet. The destruction we inflict upon Mother Earth is a result of our ignorant perception of life, and in order to heal this ignorance, we need to replace it with knowledge.

Allow the knowledge provided in this book to become the knowledge of your own mind and your own way of thinking. Allow these words to enlighten the darkest corners of yourself so that you may use your enlightenment to assist in the enlightenment of humanity. We all need to do our part of personally transforming ourselves so that we may collectively transform society. You are an integral part in this process of evolution, and humanity cannot make this change without you.

1 You

What better way to start this book then by talking about **You**. After all, this is **your** experience, and this book is focused on how **you** can unlearn **your** past conditioning and evolve **your** way of thinking. So, who are **You**? Or better yet, who do you *think* You are? When you refer to yourself as "me," or "I," what are you referring to? Are you referring to your body? Your mind? Your name? Some image you have of yourself? Do you really know?

Most people do not really know who they are. They have been told who they are, and they identify themselves with what they have been told they are—a name, a race, a social class, some role to be played in society. People cling to these beliefs for a sense of identity, and they become extremely fearful and defensive whenever their identity is questioned.

This is, of course, because they have no true sense of identity. Their identity is built upon a foundation of beliefs and concepts that have no stability in reality. The moment that they are faced with the reality that they are not who they think they are, they ignore and block out whatever information is making them feel uncomfortable, in order to restore their sense of security.

Identifying ourselves with things that have no stability makes us live in a constant state of fear. We hold onto these concepts and fear for their protection, believing that what happens to them happens to us. This way of thinking is completely delusional, and it is the biggest cause of our suffering and confusion.

To become free of this suffering, you need to understand deeply the essence of who you are, for if you knew the totality of your being you would no longer get upset over the insignificant threats to the imagined identity that you think you are.

The best way to discover who you are is by determining all of the things that you are not. Then you can disidentify with these things in order to come to a greater understanding of your true identity. Just as you peel off the layers of an onion one by one in order to reach the center, you can peel off your layers of false identification one by one until you are left with only your true self.

Let's start with the most basic form of identification: your name. This hardly deserves our attention as it is obvious to see that the reality of who you are is not confined to your name. Nonetheless, many people identify with their name and believe it to be an essential part of who they are.

How can the totality of your being be defined by a single label? Not to mention that the name you were given could have been any name. In society, we are able to communicate to one another individually by using our given names, but that does not mean we are those names. Names are just labels used to identify us, but we are not our names, and we should not identify with our names in order to get a sense of who we are.

Nor should we identify with our roles in society. You may play the role of a doctor, a waiter, a banker, a mother, a father—but these roles are not who you are. Neither are you what has happened to you in your past experiences. Many people suffer because they went through something

traumatizing in their past, and they hold onto that event and make it a part of who they are.

You are not your past. You may have been conditioned by the past, but you already existed before any of those past events happened. How could they be you? The only place that the past lives is in your memory, and if you suffer from something that happened in the past, it is because you have yet to forgive the event and let go of its emotional hold over you.

We fail to realize it in our daily lives, but there are so many things that we use to identify with. People even identify themselves with their financial status or the material items they own. Then they live in a constant state of fear and stress as they try to preserve these things in order to preserve their sense of identity. If, however, we knew our true identity, we wouldn't get so upset over these things that we have falsely identified with.

We have discussed how we are not our name, our roles in society, or our personal history, and this is not difficult to realize. But what about the body that we inhabit? Surely many people believe that their body is who they are, but is this really the truth?

2 The Body

From a very young age we are led to believe that we are this body that we inhabit, and believing this to be true, many people suffer because of what happens to their body, thinking that what happens to their body is actually happening to them. Not to mention the suffering that comes from comparing the appearance of your body to the bodies of other human beings, or the suffering that comes from those experiencing old age and the slow deterioration of the body, or those who are mistreated due to the pigmentation of the skin on their body.

This body is constantly changing. Cells are dying and being reproduced on nearly every level of your body, being fueled by the food that you eat. The body you have now is not the same body you were born with, not even close. There is not a single cell on your body that was there at the time of your birth. If this body is constantly changing, never staying the same for even a moment, how can this body be you?

And where does the line between “your body” and that which is “not your body” begin? If your body is made up of the organic matter that you consume, wouldn’t this organic matter be a part of what you call, “your body?”

Wouldn't your body be connected to the organic matter and the earth from which it came, and consequently the Universe in which the Earth exists, as well as all of the other bodies that inhabit this Universe? If your body is composed solely of the elements of the Universe, wouldn't your true body be the Universe itself?

In reality, there is only one body, and that body is the entire cosmos. An inconceivable amount of relationships are occurring between various energies and particles, giving us the illusion that there are separate entities. But all of these entities are connected to one another, made of star dust, and when the temporary relationships that form these apparently separate entities cease, these entities will return to the very same star dust from which they emerged.

Everything in the Universe is existing together, as one entity. There is no separation, no isolation, no "me" vs. "them;" there is only life, existing, moving, and evolving together. The only reason we feel like we are isolated and separate from one another is because we have been conditioned to see reality from this illogical perspective.

But this feeling of separation is just a result of our delusional perception of life. No matter how hard we try to see ourselves as separate, the truth remains that we are all one, eternally connected to each other on every level. In order to heal this sense of disconnection within ourselves, we need to heal our ignorant perception of life by replacing our ignorance with knowledge and proper understanding.

You may feel that you exist within your body, and that your body is separate from the rest of the world, but is this really true? Could you exist without the food that you eat, the air that you breathe, the water you drink, the soil that you walk on, or the sun that energizes the Earth?

So why do you view yourself as a separate entity? Your body is made up of atoms that were formed in the core of exploding stars, billions of years ago. The same particles

that form your being are connected to the particles that form my being, and the particles that form all living beings in the Universe.

According to the most accepted scientific theory, the physical Universe burst into existence from an event referred to as "The Big Bang." From that moment in time, the Universe has been continuously evolving and expanding.

Subatomic particles formed atoms and molecules, which gave rise to nebulas and galaxies, which in turn created planets capable of hosting living organisms. The entire Universe has evolved over the course of billions of years, leading up to the emergence of the human being—an organism capable of reflecting on its existence, and understanding the universal process which gave rise to its birth.

You are not separate from the Universe; you are the Universe, experiencing itself in the form of a human being—a being equipped with its own unique senses, and a nervous system to interpret these senses in order to form a unique experience of the world around it. Your experience in this form may be different than the experience of another form, for no two forms exist under the same conditions, but this does not mean that you are separate from any other forms; just your experience and perception of life are different. In truth, nothing is separate. All things are connected to the total energy of the universe, just as all waves are connected to the totality of the ocean.

3 The Mind

We may inhabit the form of a body, but this body is not who we are. If we are not our body, who are we then? Are we our minds? Are we our thoughts?

Every thought is thought in a language that you yourself did not create. The language that you think in was learned by your culture. You adopted the words that you use to define your experience, and prior to your adoption of these words, they were not a part of who you are. Your true self cannot be confined to words or defined by language.

The thoughts you think might be made of words that you did not make, but what about the thoughts themselves, the things that the words represent? What exactly is a thought?

Thoughts are a product of memory. When an experience happens, you can use thought to reflect on that experience. You can also use thought to imagine and fantasize an experience that hasn't actually happened, but your thoughts are still limited to what is known by your brain.

When you think of an event, you can only think of it in reference to what is already known to you—words, experiences, information stored in your memory. Without

any experience at all, you would have no reference, and would not be able to form a thought.

Wouldn't this display clearly that you are not your thoughts, that you had to have existed before you were able to think? Thoughts come and go, and prior to any thought at all, you still existed. We are not our thoughts, but unfortunately, many people let their thoughts control their life experience as if they really were the voice inside of their head. Their thinking is involuntary, automatically appearing in their awareness without their volition, causing their attention to be distracted by thought on a frequent basis. Some people are so identified with their involuntary thinking that the majority of their experience consists of thought, and not of awareness to what is actually happening around them.

When we think of something, we form a mental image of it, and this image is then filtered through our mental perception. How we perceive an event determines how we will experience it. If an event happens, and you perceive this event as something negative, you will create a negative mental image about that event in your mind. But this image is relative only to you. The event itself was neutral, but you perceived it as something negative, thus making it so that your experience of that event was also negative.

Our perception of reality determines our experience of reality. We hardly ever experience things as they are. Instead, we experience how we think they are; we experience our mental image of them. We do this more often than we think.

Words, for example, are nothing but symbols to represent thought forms. Think of a maple tree, standing tall in the sunlight, its vibrant green leaves spread out along its many branches, its large trunk rooted firmly into the earth. Can you see this tree? Where does the tree exist? Solely in your mind. Whatever image you see of a tree is a mental image that you yourself created. You read these words, and you used them to form an image. But is this

image life itself? Are the words that describe a maple tree anything close to an actual maple tree?

What about the words themselves: "maple tree?" Clearly this is a label for something, something we have all agreed to call by the name "maple tree," but is there such a thing? Looking at what we call a "maple tree," we see that it is made up of many other things that we have labels for—"leaves," "branches," "roots," "soil," etc. Are these each their own individual objects, or are they all a part of the same thing, being divided only by our mind-made labels?

If we label something as a "tree," does that mean that everything else is not a tree? Does that mean the tree has an existence of its own? To us it may seem that way, but is this the truth? A tree is not separate from the Earth of which it grows, nor is the Earth separate from the sky or the Universe in which it exists. The entire cosmos is connected to this thing we have labeled a "tree," showing that there really is no such thing as a "tree" in the sense that it is an object with an existence of its own. In reality, the tree is just as much a part of anything we think not to be a tree, including your own body.

The only reason we feel that a tree, a rock, a body, or anything for that matter, has an existence of its own, is because we have associated these things with our mental labels and images of them, rather than as they really are.

From the moment of birth, we have been conditioned to label objects, "table," "couch," "chair," "tree," "bird," "mom," "dad," etc.—but the labels do not explain the totality of the objects themselves. Failing to realize this, we go through life labeling our experiences, trying to categorize them with our minds, unaware that our attempt to label an experience is ultimately useless, as no label is ever capable of describing that which it attempts to define.

We do this so often, that instead of just experiencing life, we separate ourselves from life with our thoughts, and instead experience our own mental images of life, rather than life itself. Nothing in nature is separate; all things exist

together, as one. Only thoughts are capable of separating nature, but this separation exists only in our minds, and not in reality.

Living our lives in such a way has caused us to form a unique mental image and perception for nearly everything that we experience. This has gotten so out of hand that we have even formed mental images of who we are, and we then use this image of ourselves as a sense of identity, constantly worrying about its survival and its approval from others. Though our image of ourselves is not who really are, it is just an illusion that our minds have created.

4 The Ego

The ego is an imagined entity. It is a self-image created by thought, and exists only out of an identification with form. When we think of ourselves as our name, our occupation, our education, our personal history, our body, or our thoughts, we create an image of who we are. But this image is not really who we are, it is something we have made up to form a sense of identity because we are ignorant of who we really are.

This imaginary entity is what most people refer to when they speak of "I" or "me." When someone says "I am a doctor," or "I am a lawyer" and they actually believe this to be who they are, rather than just using that expression as a means of communicating their occupation, they are referring to an image they have of themselves, and confusing this self-image with their actual identity.

The problem with this is that once an image is formed, and you actually identify with that image, you have to constantly maintain that same image and fear for its protection, or else the image will cease, and you will think that somehow this means you are going to cease as well. You have confused your identity with an idea you have of yourself, and unless others acknowledge and agree upon

that idea, you will feel like your identity is threatened. Can you see the insanity in this way of thinking?

The ego is an imaginary entity created by thought, it has no solidity in reality. Therefore, people who believe they are the ego will constantly try to enforce the solidity of their ego by talking about themselves to others. They believe that if others share the same image of them, that this would strengthen their self-image, thus making it more fixed in reality.

This is why people feel the need to always talk about themselves, or even lie to others about something they have or something they have done, just so that they can strengthen their self-image.

By identifying with a mental image, people are really only separating themselves from the reality of life. Just as words and the mental images they form only isolate things from nature, trying to label yourself or form an image of who you are only separates you from everything that you really are.

If you are a doctor, does that mean that you cannot also be a father, or a mother? If you are a father or mother does that not mean you can't be an artist or a business owner? What about a scientist or author? Would any of these labels actually represent the reality of who you are? Of course not, yet for some reason we cling to these labels for a sense of identity. We cling to them because they allow us to form an image of ourselves, and then we can mentally label and understand that image.

But we are not our image of ourselves, nor can we understand who we are with our limited language and thought. The reality of who you are is beyond comprehension. Therefore, in order to know who you are, you have to give up trying to comprehend who you are. This may seem paradoxical, but there is a difference between knowing, and comprehending.

You know how to breathe, but you don't comprehend the process of breathing—how your lungs inflate and

deflate, or how they deliver oxygen to your bloodstream. You know how to walk, but you don't comprehend the actual muscle contractions that are allowing the body to move, or the electrical signal being sent from the brain to the nerves of your legs.

In the same way, you can know who you are, without being able to define who you are or confine the totality of your being to some mind-made words and concepts. You know who you are because you are; because you exist. You do not need a reason to be. Just be.

In order to come to the truth of who you are, you have to let go of the mind's desire to comprehend, label, and organize everything. The mind does this because it wants to have control over its experience. If the mind doesn't comprehend something, it thinks that it has no way to influence or control it, and this makes it feel inferior, or perhaps even afraid. But do you ever really have control of anything? We like to think that we do, especially if we are identified with our mind and its thoughts, but in reality, we have very little control over anything that happens in nature.

If you wanted to, you could get up and walk to the nearest store. You might have control over that decision, but do you consciously control the movement of your legs with every step? Do you control the inhalation and exhalation of your breath? Do you control the flow of your blood, the digestion of your food, or any of the subconscious activities that your body performs? These things seem to just happen on their own without your control. You have very little involvement in these activities.

You may decide to walk to the store, but can you determine exactly what will happen on this walk? You may have an expectation of what will happen—some image you hold in your mind—but it is unlikely that your expectation will match exactly what happens. Anything could happen during that short walk to the store. You have no control over what happens.

Realizing this, it may bring you peace to simply let go of trying to control things, and instead allow things to happen naturally. The only things that you have control over are your own actions, and your own state of being. Anything else is completely out of your control, and stressing over it is useless, as things will happen how they happen regardless.

Rather than being so focused on controlling what happens, focus more on choosing how you react to what happens. Any situation in life is neutral, and only your thoughts about that situation can make you happy or sad. It is your way of thinking and perceiving that determines how you feel about an event.

We only try to control what happens because we think that we can influence life to work in our favor. This is another delusional thought produced by the ego. The ego stresses over events because the ego is worried about its survival. The ego wants to maintain its solidity in the world by constantly strengthening its self-image. If something does not go according to the ego's plan, the ego feels that it is threatened and begins to fear for its protection.

You can observe this in someone very easily when they are attached to a certain belief, and they defensively protect that belief whenever it is threatened, ignoring any information that opposes their belief, because they need that belief in order to have a sense of identity.

For example, the Christian who cannot have an open conversation about other religious beliefs, or the Republican who cannot consider a Democrat's point of view. These people cling to the concept of being a Christian, or Republican, and they use these beliefs to form a sense of identity. They cannot question their beliefs without questioning their identity, and when their identity is questioned, they feel threatened and defensively protect their identity. This, of course, is all a result of the ego.

Our identification with the ego is the cause of our suffering—both individually and as a society. Individually,

the ego makes us suffer by causing us to think that we are victims of our experience. When we are strongly identified with the ego, we don't see everything as one big happening that we are a part of. Instead, we think everything is happening directly to us, and perceive everything as some form of personal attack.

We feel that there is a "me" that is personally offended; our self-image has been threatened, and consequently we feel like we have been wronged. Nothing happens directly to you. Everything is just happening, and you are an integral part of this happening.

If someone tries to make fun of you, you can either perceive that as a direct attack on you personally (most people do), or you can see that situation for what it really is—someone attempting to strengthen their self-image by belittling yours. It is nothing to take personally; their actions have nothing to do with you. They are simply reflecting their own insecurities.

If someone judges other people, it is because they judge themselves. They haven't accepted who they are, and so they have to point out the flaws of others so that the others can appear unacceptable, too. This is just one of the many tricks that the ego plays in order to maintain its self-image and its sense of identity.

Living in a society dominated by ego, the many individual egos give rise to a collective ego. People then identify themselves with their nation, their religion, their politics, etc.—all of which are only concepts created by the minds of humans. Because of this collective ego, people will allow such atrocities as war or genocide to occur, because they believe that they have enemies that threaten their sense of collective identity.

In truth, not only are they connected to those they call their "enemies," but they depend on having "enemies" in order to feel like they belong to a special group of people. How could someone identify with the "good side" unless there were a "bad side" to compare themselves to? This

happens on so many different scales of reality. People will discriminate against "blacks" in order to belong to their group of "whites;" the "rich" will discriminate from the "poor" in order to feel superior to those with less financial wealth.

You can also observe this in the person who is overly proud and defensive of their country. Perhaps even you have some sense of pride for your country and defensively protect your country's image. This is deep down of course just a way of protecting your own image, because you have been raised to identify with that image.

A country is just a concept. A largely agreed upon concept, nonetheless it is still a concept, it is still mind-made, meaning it is ultimately not real. Believing that you belong to a country causes you to feel like you are somehow separate from those who don't belong to your country, and it also causes you to feel like it is okay to harm those who belong to a different country because they are not connected to you or the group you feel like you belong to. Unfortunately, this also happens frequently with those who identify with a certain religion.

Again, this is just another delusional thought process formed by the ego that causes us to perceive separation in an interconnected Universe. It is this delusional perception that produces so many disasters, all in the name of benefiting oneself at the expense of others, failing to see that the "others" are not different from what one refers to as one's "self."

So much suffering is caused by this delusional belief that we are separate from one another. So much death, so much violence, so much destruction, all because people are identified with their mental images, and are unaware of the reality of who they are.

Can you observe the ego in yourself? Can you become aware of the things that you cling to for a sense of identity? Can you see the concepts or beliefs that you hold onto, the things that make you feel like you belong, or the things that make you feel like you are somehow separate from others?

Can you acknowledge the image you have created of yourself? Can you see how this image exists only in your mind? Are you aware of all of the things that you do or have done in the name of maintaining this social image? Can you recall the times that you have lied, or bragged about your experience, just to improve your self-image in the eyes of others?

What would happen if you stopped trying to maintain this image? What would happen if you no longer felt the tendency to protect your image, enforce your opinions, or defend your beliefs, and instead just let go of this tendency and allowed life to happen? Would you cease to exist? Would you vanish along with your self-image?

No, of course not. Yet, this is how people behave. They believe that their image is who they are, and if their image were to stop existing, that somehow would mean they would stop existing.

The ego is produced by any identification with form. When you identify with a form of any kind, whether it is a physical form like the body, or a mental form like thoughts, beliefs, and other concepts, you are really just strengthening the ego in you. You are strengthening the idea of who you are, and are consequently separating yourself from the reality of your being.

If, however, you realize that you are not any of the things that you identify with, and instead let go of your attachment to these things, all that will be left is you—the real you—the awareness that is your true nature.

5 Consciousness

We live in a universe of forms. We inhabit the physical forms of our bodies, we dwell on the physical form of the Earth, and we think in the mental forms of thoughts, feelings, and words.

Everything that we experience is only possible due to the world of form. Although every form that exists is undergoing continuous change. There is nothing in the world of form that remains permanent.

Billions of cells in our body die every minute, being replaced by the new cells we obtain through the food we eat. Atoms and molecules are colliding and exchanging patterns of energy on every scale of reality. Everything is in a constant state of vibration, endlessly moving, dancing, and changing.

Time is the only reason that forms appear to have any solidity at all, but the true nature of all forms is impermanence; formlessness. When we fail to realize the formless and ever-changing nature of the Universe, we cling to forms for a sense of security and identity, and this attachment to form is the root cause of our suffering.

We cling to the forms of our bodies, believing that these bodies are who we are. But how can you be your

body when the body you have now is not at all the same body you had at birth, during childhood, a year ago, or even a day ago?

We cling to the mental forms of our beliefs, thoughts, and opinions, believing that our mind is what makes us who we are. But everything that makes up your mind is the result of your past conditioning, your experiences, your circumstances, the information you have obtained, the events that your mind has witnessed and documented in the form of memory. Who were you before your mind had been conditioned to view life as it now sees it?

Everything in the Universe is constantly changing, nothing remains the same for even a moment. There is no solidity, there are no permanent forms, no enduring entities; there is only one vast universal process continually changing, moving, and evolving together.

All forms are composed of other forms. A body is made up of atoms, cells, microbes, bones, tissues, muscles, nerves, etc. These forms that make up your body can only exist because of the other forms that fuel them—the plants, air, and water of the Earth, the heat, light and energy of the sun. There is no thing that exists in itself; all things are connected, a part of the same ever changing event that we call life.

If everything that has an apparent form is in truth formless, wouldn't the true nature of the Universe itself then be formless? If everything with form is constantly undergoing change, then where does that leave you? Who are you if you are not any of the forms that you have been conditioned to identify with?

You are the formless awareness in which all forms exist. Forms come and go, but the awareness that witnesses and experiences form is always present. Throughout every one of life's experiences, there is always an awareness present, there is always YOU here to perceive these forms and turn them into your reality. If there were no awareness how could anything exist at all?

Who would be there to experience existence?

You are not any of the things that happen in your experience, you are the witness of experience. You are the awareness in which experience happens, the consciousness that allows any experience to exist at all. Without you, there could be no experience.

6 Illusion and Truth

The concept of Form and Formless is relatively the same as the spiritual concept of Illusion and Truth. The Truth is simply that which is definite, enduring, lasting, and permanent. Illusions are things that are fleeting, temporary, changing, and impermanent. If something is undergoing constant change and transformation how can it be the Truth which is permanent and undying?

Illusions are still very real, but they are short-lived, transient, and changing, therefore they are not the Truth, which is long-lasting, infinite, and eternal. Being able to distinguish between Illusion and Truth enables us to understand the ways in which our minds tend to cling to illusions for a sense of security and identity, an act which is inevitably futile.

Everything in the world of form is impermanent, and thus, belongs also to the world of illusion. A tree may exist as a tree now, but has it always been a tree? Before it was a tree it was a seed, it was the soil, the rain, the clouds, the earth, and the sky, and these many elements still live through the tree, and as the tree. The idea that a tree has an existence of its own is an illusion, as is seeing anything as a separate and fixed entity.

There can be no tree without the many elements that make what we call a "tree," just as there can be none of these elements without the many other elements that make up them. Everything is a part of the same ever-changing process. There is nothing permanent in the world of form and illusion.

This concept is simple enough to grasp when studying things you believe to be outside of yourself, like a tree, but can you allow yourself to study the same phenomena within yourself?

Can you look into your body, and see that its existence is maintained solely by things you believe to be not your body—food, air, water, sunlight, space? Can you look into the many things that you use to identify with and see their illusory nature?

Can you see your name as just a label given to you by society? Can you see your occupation, your beliefs, your opinions, your race, your genetic history, or your relationships as just information and experiences that you have adopted during your development? Who were you before all of this?

We play many roles in life, and we seem to have many different characters that we identify with for a sense of security, but who are you in these roles? Who is the one that is acting out the parts of these many different characters? It's easy to observe the illusion of permanence in nature, but it takes a great degree of honesty and courage to look within oneself and see the illusions that lie within.

What is it that you identify with? Your social class, your religion, your family, your race, your body? Do you really feel like any of these ultimately define the totality of who you are?

Part of the reason most people do not look into this is because they have been conditioned to identify with these many different roles in life; their attention is so extraverted that they are hardly aware of the subtle nature of their own mind. Although an even deeper reason that people do not

look into the roles they identify with is because they are afraid to discover that these roles are not who they are.

People live their entire lives on the foundation that they are a Christian, a Muslim, a Banker, a Doctor, a Man, a Woman, etc. They cling so tightly to these conceptual roles for a sense of identity, that any time their identity is questioned they defensively protect their beliefs and avoid the situation in order to feel secure and comfortable again.

The roles that we identify with in life are impermanent, and as mentioned before, even this body is impermanent. If these roles are temporary, relative, and constantly changing, how can they be the Truth of who you are? Can you see that identifying with these roles is just identification with an illusion?

Perhaps you can see the transitory nature of these roles, but going one step further, can you understand the same transitory nature of your thoughts and feelings as well? This is usually where the most resistance is felt by those inquiring into their nature. They can peel back the layers of illusion with little struggle, until they are faced with the task of inquiring into the illusory nature of their own thoughts.

Most people are strongly identified with their thoughts, and believe that the voice in their head is who they are. But if you are the voice inside of your head, who is the one that is aware of this voice?

It is so subtle that it requires a great deal of attention and awareness to truly understand it, but you are not your thoughts, you are the witness of your thoughts. You are consciousness.

When identified with thought and emotion, people view themselves as separate from the world, they feel like they are victims of their circumstances and the actions of others, constantly focused on "me" and "my" problems. But there is no "I" in this sense.

There are no separate entities, as we are all connected to each other and the greater whole of the universe. One of the greatest ways of maintaining this illusion of separation is by finding faults in others, blaming others, and seeing others as enemies.

By putting the blame on others, or trying to gain victory over others, one strengthens the identity of a separate self, and makes oneself feel as if he or she is superior. Though even in this scenario one needs the "other" in order to feel good about oneself. You depend just as much on the others as you do yourself, for without them you would have no sense of self.

But in truth, there are no others. There are only various organisms with brains that have been conditioned to see separation amongst themselves, and it is this view of separation that causes us to act violently toward each other, and toward the planet with which we are deeply intertwined.

How did the existence of this form (body) come to be? It came from the Earth, from the raw materials of matter, the energy of life, and the intimate process of evolution that allowed it to advance to such a stage. Within you still exists these fundamental building blocks of creation, the physical matter of nature, the energy that flows throughout the Universe, and the essence of life in your being, my being, and every being.

The entire Universe is composed of the same materials, and on a quantum level we can easily observe just how connected we are. There is no boundary separating one particle from the next, no wall that divides "you" from "me," or "us" from "them." These are just illusions that our minds have created, illusions that we have mistakenly identified with due to our ignorant perception of life.

Thoughts are nothing but labels—words that we have adopted from our society. We can rearrange these labels in different ways to form some sense of personalization to them, but your thoughts are not personal to you, they are bound to the culture that created the language in which you think.

You are not “I,” or “me;” those are just words that attempt to define a greater reality. But words are limited, they are forms, and they can never accurately define the true nature of the Universe or of your own being, which is formless and unlimited.

Thoughts and words can be a very effective form of communicating and expressing things to one another, but they are still just thoughts and words. They are not and cannot ever amount to the reality of that which they attempt to define.

So then how do we understand the reality of nature, and of our own being? We have to learn to step out of the realm of thought and mental imagery, and move beyond into the realm of this moment. We have to stop thinking, and practice being.

Don’t misunderstand what I am saying here: thoughts and words are a necessary part of life, especially since we have created a society that is dependent upon them, but should they take up the majority of our time and experience? Should we allow them to completely control our lives and make us suffer?

It may be hard to realize the error in our way of thinking when we have been unconscious of the nature of thought for nearly our entire lives, but our addiction to labeling, defining, and conceptualizing every event has separated us from the reality of life. We now live in the realm of our individual thoughts, rather than in the collective realm of being and living.

Hardly anyone is present to life as it is happening now. Each person seems to be living in their own mental world, creating their own mental problems, completely ignorant to the reality of this moment.

Can you see the error in this way of living? Thoughts are subjective to each person’s mind. They are indeed thought in a language that is shared, but they are unique to each person’s perception, circumstances, and experience.

The present moment, life as it is happening now, is something that is shared by everybody. When living in the realm of our thoughts, we feel separate and isolated because we are creating this division within ourselves. When one steps out of the realm of thought, however, they step into the realm of this moment, a moment that is free from thought and personal opinions, one that affects everyone and everything, a moment that we are all involved in, even if we choose to be ignorant of what is happening in this moment.

This moment is the true reality of life. Our thoughts just create a personalized filter of illusion over life, and we then experience our mind's illusions rather than the reality of what is happening now.

When one understands deeply how we are all living as one, bound eternally to the present moment, they can see clearly how there is no separation, how all things are shared, and how all of us are interconnected to one another and to the Earth on which we live. They can also see how humanity is living under a type of mental psychosis, an identification with thought and illusion, blinding them from the reality of life.

Those who wake up from this illusion and step outside of their conditioned mind experience a profound realization of truth, and it is this realization that redirects most people onto a path of spiritual understanding and meaning, rather than one of ignorance and self-induced suffering.

Perhaps you have had glimpses of this truth as well. Our entire lives we have been subconsciously conditioned to identify ourselves with thought, and the moment we step out of this realm of compulsive thinking, however brief it may be, we enter into the vast realm of life, where such mind-made illusions as hatred, violence, blame, depression, anxiety, fear, etc., seem to have no value, and all that we experience is total freedom, peace, and love for existence.

Those who undergo such a profound awakening never forget the experience, although unfortunately, they have

such a powerful momentum of conditioned thought in their minds that most are easily pulled back into the illusory reality of their own opinions, beliefs, judgments and perceptions.

Some are able to feel this freedom from thought in experiences that involve intense sensory stimulation, such as skydiving, snowboarding, or other extreme sports. When we step out of the realm of thought we feel alive, we feel free from the pressure of living confined to our mental prisons, and we experience a great sense of peace and joy.

There are other and more effective ways to be free of your mental prison, but they require your honesty, attention, and willingness to let go of old beliefs. It requires that you observe within yourself the many illusions that you identify with, including your own thoughts, so that you may become aware of your true nature as the witness of these illusions. It requires that you look deeply within yourself to discover the truth of who you are.

7 Observing Your Own Mind

It's easy to point out the faults in others, or to blame others for their behavior, but can you observe the faults in your own way of thinking? In your own behavior? We often judge others because of our own insecurities. This is an unconscious act of course, or else it is unlikely that we would continue to do it. We see someone with a weird haircut or strange clothes and in our minds we judge them for that. Why? Because we are insecure about our own appearance, and pointing out the flaws in others takes the attention away from our own shortcomings.

We are only making them seem like less so that we can feel like more, so that we can feel validated and superior. It is the same as labeling one group of people as "bad" so that we can belong to the group of people who are "good." Though neither group can exist without the other.

How can you have good without bad? How can there be hot without cold? Light without dark? Or self without other? We can only know one with reference to the other, showing that there isn't really an "other," neither are separate, they are one. Duality is an illusion.

There are many people on a spiritual path that still let themselves be guided by the ego. They pursue the spiritual

path because they had a glimpse of what exists beyond the ego, but end up strengthening their ego by clinging to spirituality for a sense of identity. They feel as if they belong to some kind of "spiritual" group, and would have no sense of belonging without reference to those who do not share their same understanding of life.

They are still one with those whom they view as separate from them, only their minds are conditioned to perceive reality differently. Often people in this class will cling to things that strengthen their sense of spirituality—crystals, spiritual music, stimulating scents and herbs, psychedelics, etc.—but this is still just extroverting their attention and keeping them distracted from observing the ego within themselves.

These things are all beneficial and wonderful things that can aid one on a spiritual path, but the real spiritual work happens within. It comes from being aware of the patterns that your mind has formed due to its conditioning, and retraining the mind to perceive life in a more natural and wholesome way.

It is a process of unlearning, of unconditioning, detangling the web of thought patterns that form your perception of life, and replacing them with new patterns based on truth. It involves letting go of the illusions that you have identified with in the past in order to come to a greater realization of who you really are.

You are not your thoughts or emotions. You are not the one that thinks, "I am suffering, I have been wronged, I am this or I am that," you are the one that is aware of your thoughts and emotions. You are the "I Am." You are the consciousness in which these sensations arise. You are the witness that lies in the background of thought, the very essence of life itself.

The more that you understand your identity as awareness, the less you identify with the impermanent forms that arise in your awareness, and the less you suffer. You suffer less because you realize that these forms are

not who you are, and thus you have no reason to stress over them or try to control them. You can leave them as they are. You let them come, let them go, and let them be.

Suddenly, all the pressure you felt to achieve, to become, to gain, and accomplish, ceases, and you are left with the simple joy of being alive. You cease clinging to life and begin allowing life to happen through you. You realize that everything you had been seeking was within you all along. You already are that which you were striving to become, only your mind was attempting to find who you were in other things, rather than in the natural essence of your being.

An essential part of coming to this realization is letting go of the need to define it or understand it. Words are limited, and they are not fully capable of defining the totality of who you are. When you let yourself simply "be" without trying to understand it, you are left with who you are in your natural state, and who you are then becomes easily understood.

Consciousness—your true self—is subjective. It is an awareness, a presence, it is the essence of life itself. You cannot define this subjective experience by turning it into an object—a word, a label, a thought, or a mental image. Consciousness is not something outside of yourself that you can study, it is who you are. You cannot be conscious of your consciousness any more than you can lick your own tongue, see your own eyes, or cut a knife with its own blade.

Once you see that comprehending your formless nature is ultimately impossible, then you can let go of trying to understand consciousness, and can simply be consciousness. Then, suddenly, your existence as consciousness becomes completely understood. You are the awareness that is always present, preceding every thought, event, and experience that happens. You are not the mind that seeks for understanding; you are the witness of this mind—the awareness that lies in the background, always observing, yet never observed.

The mind clings to concepts and labels for a sense of understanding; a sense of control. But this tendency to cling to life will only cut you off from life. It is like holding your breath while refusing to exhale. Eventually you will suffocate, unless you are willing to let go.

Let go of the need to know, the need to define life and categorize it in your mind. Simply let life be, and let yourself be. Realize the limitations of the mind, and understand that you are not the mind, and that your existence can never be understood by the mind. It has to be felt to be known. You have to detach from your mind so that it no longer controls your experience.

The primary thing to understand here is that you are the witness, you are awareness; you are not your thoughts. So if you can practice observing your thoughts, especially while in the midst of thoughts that seem to take away your peace, you have already taken the most important step. You have made the unconscious conscious; you have replaced thought with awareness.

You will never come to know yourself by thinking about your existence—by clinging to conceptual or material forms—for awareness is formless, and no amount of form will ever be able to describe your formless nature. At best, forms can only point you in the direction to discover the truth within yourself.

You cannot understand this by thinking, but by being—by feeling, existing, and living. Thoughts only separate us from the present moment, and consequently from life, since the dimension of life and the present moment are one and the same. Once you understand the futility of thought, then you can move beyond it. Then you can enter the realm of no-thought, of being without thinking. This is where the essence of life is understood.

Can you simply be? That is, can you simply sit and exist, without trying to label or define your experience? Try it. You may be able to get a glimpse of what it is like to simply be, but the experience is unlikely to last for more than a

brief moment. Before you know it, the thinking mind makes its way back into your awareness, and you begin labeling, defining, conceptualizing, and fantasizing once again.

Although, if you were able to get a glimpse of what it is like to simply be, that is all that is needed to prove that you are not your thoughts. Thoughts of "I am this," or "I am that,"—the illusions you identify with—are shown to be exactly that—illusions—created solely by your mind and its thinking.

Once you see a glimpse of what it is like to move beyond thought and into being, you are capable of creating a gap between you and your thoughts, and the more you practice, the larger the gap becomes.

You begin to see the illusory nature of thought as your thoughts fade away one by one. Thoughts lose their seriousness and stability, and you realize that they are only thoughts, and that they are not life itself. No matter how much you think about a situation it will never define the situation as it really is, but only how you perceive it.

Can you observe this insistent need to constantly think? Can you see it in yourself? Can you acknowledge your attachment to thought, and can you become aware of how your thoughts are separating you from this moment? From life? Can you become conscious of the unconsciousness in you? That is to say, can you replace your unconscious thinking with your conscious awareness?

The more you practice being aware of thought, the more you understand that you are not your thoughts, and no matter how much you choose to think about yourself, your thoughts will never be able to define the essence of who you are.

Practice being the witness. Watch your thoughts, create the gap between them and your awareness. Simply sit and observe, focusing only on your breath and your awareness. The thoughts will still come, but do not let them distract you. Take the thoughts lightly, they are only thoughts, and there is no need to follow each thought to its end.

The moment a thought arises, simply acknowledge it, smile to it, and let it go. Return to your natural state of being: awareness.

The longer you sit in this state of mental calmness and alertness, the stronger this state will become. Eventually the habit to remain grounded in this state will form, causing this to be your natural state.

Your thoughts are not going to disappear; they have an entire lifetime of momentum which causes them to arise out of habit, but the more you replace thought with awareness, the more capacity you have for being present without thought interfering, and naturally you will think less and less. And when thoughts do arise, they do not consume you. You realize they are just thoughts and you do not have to take them seriously.

Thought is a product of the past. It is made up of information and memory, functioning solely by relating the moment to what has already been recorded by the brain. But life is new, it is fluid, moving, always changing. It cannot be understood with reference to the old. It can only be experienced as it exists now.

Look at the rivers and streams of the earth, they flow with whatever crosses their path. They do not resist their natural flow. Why is it that we insist on making life difficult? Why can we not flow with life and live naturally in each moment? Why must we resist life, and cause our own suffering in the process?

If you are suffering emotionally, it is because you are resisting the flow of life. You are clinging to your thoughts about a person, object, or situation. You are allowing your own mind to make you suffer.

Your failure to let go of a situation is simply your failure to let go of your thoughts. You are still holding on because you want to know more, you want closure, an explanation, an apology, or whatever the case might be. But is this way of thinking making you happy? No. it is the reason you are unhappy.

You are not miserable because of the event that happened. You are miserable because of your thoughts about the event that happened. Stop resisting. Accept the past. Forgive the past. Let go of the past so that you can be at peace now. The past has already let go of you; it lives only in your thoughts, it is no longer the reality of this moment.

What will it take for you to accept the past and move on? Do you really need an explanation, reconciliation, or justification? What will happen if you simply stopped thinking about it? What would happen if you chose to stop thinking in general? Would you die? Would you cease to exist? No, of course not. Then why must you cling to thought as if your life depended on it? Can you let go of thought altogether and simply be?

If you can, you will discover that peace is available to you. It has always been available to you. Only your unconscious attachment to thought has caused you to suffer.

If you want to suffer, continue to let thought guide and control your life unconsciously. But if you want to be at peace, break free from the prison of your obsessive thinking by entering into the realm of this moment, into the realm of awareness, into the realm of life. Replace thinking with being, become aware of your thoughts, and do not let thoughts take away your peace.

If you can reconnect with this state of pure awareness within you, and can truly feel and know this to be your true being, an amazing thing will happen. You will realize that the ultimate truth of life is your existence, and that everything else is merely a projection of your own awareness.

It is such a strange thing to realize, that you might just burst out in laughter the moment that you have the realization. Everything that exists is merely a projection of awareness. Your life, your experience, your story—it is all being created and maintained by you. Whatever happens in your experience is your own making.

For example, it seems to you that you are reading these words on a computer screen or a piece of paper, but is this true? In reality, signals of light are being picked up by your eyes, and sent along the optic nerve to the back of your brain where vision takes place. Really, what you are seeing "out here" is a projection of what is "in here"—a projection of what the nerves inside of your head are doing.

The same is true for any of your senses—sight, sound, touch, taste, smell—your body is just picking up vibrations from the Universe and using these vibrations to form a sense of experience. At the root of all this experience is you, the awareness that turns these vibrations into an experience. However you choose to perceive reality is how you will experience it. Your experience is your creation.

But if you are awareness, and the entire universe is just a projection of awareness, what does that mean for other people? What does that mean for my friends, and family? For my dog, or for my plants? Don't they have an awareness of their own? Would they be a part of this projection called reality? Or would they be a part of the projector: consciousness?

8 Life

The same awareness that exists in you exists in me, your parents, your relatives, your friends, your pets, and every living thing in existence. Our apparently many forms are really just a manifestation of the one formless consciousness.

Look into the eyes of another being: can you not see the same source of life staring back at you? Consciousness is not dull and lifeless; it is living, it is aware, it is intelligent and blissful. Consciousness is the spirit of life that is expressing itself in the world of form—through my form, your form, and through all forms.

Consciousness is the substance of creation. There is the personal experience of consciousness that each being has—this is what people often refer to as the soul—and there is the omnipresent consciousness which is the total field of consciousness itself—the spirit. The soul is just a temporary manifestation of the spirit. It is consciousness inhabiting form. It still has its roots in the total field of consciousness, just as every tree has its roots in the total field of the earth.

On the surface, it may appear that we exist independently of the other souls around us, but this is just

an illusion. Beneath the surface we are all connected, a part of the one eternal spirit of consciousness itself.

This omnipresent consciousness—the spirit of life itself inhabiting every being, is what religion has often referred to as "God." According to Christianity, God made man in his image—another way of saying that humans are just a reflection of the total spirit of life.

Religion is a human attempt to interpret the reality of life, but life cannot be confined to words or scriptures. Life is something that has to be lived to be understood. No definition of "life," or "spirit," or "God," can ever amount to the reality of what these words are attempting to define. But if you let go of trying to define life, and simply feel the essence of life within you, and see this essence of life in everyone else, then you understand the truth of existence. Then you can see that we are all one consciousness experiencing itself. There is no separation—separation is an illusion—there is only oneness, only the one spirit manifesting itself in every temporary form, all of which will inevitably return to the same spirit from which they emerged.

You cannot see this when you are separated from life, living in the realm of your conditioned thoughts and mental imagery, because your current level of understanding was produced by a society that is ignorant to this ultimate truth of life. You can only see this truth when you are totally present to life—aware of this moment, flowing with the current of this moment, and allowing this moment to unfold naturally, rather than resisting the moment by desiring it to be different.

When you are present to this moment, you see the spirit manifested in all its forms. You see life in everything that exists. You see the very same essence of life in you living through all beings, and you also see that everything you perceive and experience is occurring within the field of your consciousness.

We have been taught to view life as something exclusive to some, and unavailable to others, but is this true? Is life confined to a few forms and not to all forms? Is there anything that exists separately from life? What is it that defines the living from the apparently nonliving?

Is it movement that determines the living from the nonliving? Your body can move, but would you call a plant that is not moving "dead"? Is it growth then? Plants grow, but so do mountains, rivers, fires, and even galaxies. If your body stops growing, does that mean that it is dead?

A rock might not seem like it is alive because our senses are too limited to observe any kind of movement or change. But if we were to use a scientific instrument to enhance our senses, we could easily see that at the molecular, atomic, and subatomic levels, that rock is vibrating, pulsating, and moving.

Is our distinction between that which is living and that which is not living a matter of more or less movement? What is it that causes this movement, that creates the illusion that certain things are living and others are nonliving? We might call it energy, chi, prana, or whatever label we wish to give to it, but it is essentially the life-force of the universe, a force that is eternally present, a force that, if nonexistent, would be unable to create any forms whatsoever.

Life is not something that is confined to beings with sensory organs, it is the energy that creates, organizes, and destroys these beings, along with all other things. The energy of life expresses itself through you, through me, and through all forms. There is no distinction between that which is living and that which is nonliving. It is all just life. The Universe is one living and interconnected event, an event that is so vast, and so inclusive, that no single brain can comprehend it in its totality. We can only know it by discovering its essence within ourselves.

9 Love

If the entire Universe is composed of the same life energy, and at the source of this energy lies the one omnipresent consciousness, what exactly does this mean for us? What does it mean that the same energy that makes up my being, makes up your being, that my awareness is your awareness, that we are all connected?

It means that the ideas we have of being separate from one another, the beliefs we use as a justification for harming the planet, or for acting selfishly, are nothing more than illusions produced by our ignorant perception of life. It means that in reality, we are all connected to life, and that harming any life harms all life, including "your" life. It means that when anyone acts violently towards another, they are really acting violently towards themselves. It means that no matter how we choose to perceive the world, the truth remains that we are bound to one another, and to all of creation, for all of existence is a manifestation of the same primordial spirit of consciousness.

We have no choice but to love one another, look after one another, and take care of one another. When you see someone suffering, it is really you suffering in the form

of that person. And when you compassionately send your love and care to that person, you are contributing that loving energy to all that exists.

Love is the profound connection we feel when we realize our oneness with others, when you look into the eyes of another person and realize that person is you. Every being comes from the same life essence as you; they are the same consciousness, just inhabiting a different form.

Whether you are looking into the eyes of another human, a dog, a fish, or an insect, or whether you are feeling the presence of life in a plant, in the soil, or in a mineral, it is all the same consciousness inhabiting a different form. Everything is you.

You don't exist in the Universe; you are so intertwined with the Universe that you can be nothing but the Universe itself. Your true nature is consciousness, and this consciousness is connected to the consciousness of the Universe. Doing harm to any one of consciousness's manifestations—whether it be another person, animal, or plant—is essentially only causing harm to yourself.

All humans, animals, and plants are made up of cells that are alive and conscious. Their consciousness is arguably far more simple than our own, but it must exist at some level because they perform tasks and respond to their environment. They know that they must be doing whatever it is they are driven to do, but they do not see that billions of them come together to create a human, a plant, or an animal.

In the same way, we are so focused on living our own individual lives that we are unaware we make up an entire organism called "Earth," and that we are its many cells, living together as one. Although currently, we behave as if we are a virus to the earth, slowly destroying the organism that we are a part of, rather than ensuring its health and survival. This is of course a result of our ignorance and our failure to see how we and the Earth are one.

The Universe, The Earth, our bodies, animals, plants, minerals, cells—we are layer upon layer of the universe experiencing itself as separate entities that are really all one and the same.

To use an analogy: The Universe is a tree, and we are all its leaves. Each leaf is kept alive by the total energy of the tree, but from its own perspective, the leaf seems as if it were separate from the rest of the leaves, and even the tree itself. And what spiritual teachers refer to as "Enlightenment" is simply the realization that the leaf is connected to the tree as a whole, as are all of the leaves, and that the true nature of the leaf is the entire tree. The leaf cannot be without the tree. In reality, there is no separation.

Love is the feeling that we have when we can see that we are not separate from the other leaves, that we are all creations of the tree from which we emerged. When you can see another as a reflection of yourself, then you have compassion for them, and this kind of compassion for others is what is truly needed to heal the world.

We never really know the circumstances that others are experiencing. But knowing that we have suffered, enables us to see that others suffer just like we do. People often hide their suffering and look as if they are not suffering on the surface, but deep down they may be in great pain. Knowing that everyone experiences suffering in their own way, should inspire us to do our best to free people from their suffering, to be kind to others at all times, because even the smallest act of kindness can feel like a breath of fresh air to someone who is suffocating from their suffering.

We cannot continue to exist with so much violence, so much disrespect, so much fear and judgment toward others; we are only hurting ourselves by doing this. Our actions ripple out into the Universe, creating a chain of events that affects every single particle in existence. Actions driven by love benefit more than just us or those in direct contact with our actions, they benefit the entire Universe.

Any actions that are driven by fear, violence, anger, hatred, jealousy, or greed, are produced by a mind that is dominated by ego. If we realized our connection to one another and to the source of life, we would act only in love, always having the health of life as a whole in mind.

In order to feel the love that comes from understanding our oneness, we have to let go of the idea that we are separate, we have to see clearly that we are not the ego, the ego is just a thought that the brain, and by extension the Universe, is having. To say it from a Christian's perspective: We must surrender ourselves (our ideas of being a separate self) in order to receive the love of God.

The notion that we are separate from the rest of existence causes us to cling to life out of fear. We cling to the world because we fail to realize that we are the world, and it is this ignorant perception of life that has produced our misconception of what love really is.

Many people confuse love with attachment, which is a quality of fear—the fear of loss—and it results in insecurity and dependency, which has been the cause of many broken hearts and failed relationships.

The qualities of fear are attachment, dependency, and resistance. The qualities of love are appreciation, understanding, and acceptance. We can observe very easily in our personal relationships whether we are acting out of fear or love.

Looking at an intimate relationship with a partner for example, if we are selfish, clingy, jealous, spiteful, mistrusting, dependent, etc., our relationship is composed primarily of fear or ego. If, however we are selfless, understanding, accepting, appreciative, caring, supporting and trusting, our relationship is composed primarily of love or spirit.

All emotions are essentially produced by feelings of either fear or love; either seeing ourselves as the ego—separate; or understanding our existence as spirit—connected.

Fear and our idea of separation produce feelings of attachment, resistance, anxiety, anger, violence, hatred, jealousy, envy, and depression. Love and our understanding of oneness produce feelings of freedom, acceptance, security, calmness, peace, understanding, gratitude, trust, compassion, and happiness.

Observe within yourself whether your relationships are driven by fear or love. Do you really love the other person in the relationship? Meaning, do you really want what is best for them, regardless of whether that involves you in their life? Or do you just wish to control this person for your own benefit? If your love is only a will to possess, it is not love.

Observe how you interact with other human beings, animals, and plants. Do you care for these living beings or do you just wish to use them for your benefit, and otherwise have no interest or care at all? Do you judge others based on their appearance or the form they inhabit? They cannot help the way they look, and the way they look has nothing to do with who they really are. What sense does it make to judge someone because they look, think, or behave differently than you? What benefit do you get from that? None. Only the ego benefits from judgment by enforcing its idea of separation and strengthening its self-image. But you are not the ego, and the views of separation that stem from a mind dominated by ego are not composed of love.

Love is not controlling. Love is not restricting, limiting, or exclusive. Love is free. Love is relaxing, sincere, and inclusive. Love is the energy that we need to embody in order to heal the planet, society, and ourselves.

We need to align our state of being with love in order to find peace. We must let go of the conditioning that has caused us to act from a view of ego and separation, and begin acting from an understanding of love, connection, and oneness. Love is the only thing that is truly capable of healing the state of the world.

10 Mindfulness

Society is lacking in love; lacking in care for one another, lacking in respect for one another, and lacking in real social depth and connection between one another. We do not treat each other with love, and respect each other as human beings. Most people only interact on the surface, speaking of superficial topics that neither person has any real interest in.

Humans are social creatures, and we long for more depth, more connection, more expression. Unfortunately, everyone is so dominated by their minds and their egos that they don't interact with their hearts. Our interactions are dull, usually consisting of pointless dialogue and whatever topics are popular in today's media.

Because of this, we feel alienated from one another. We are unable to express ourselves because we fear what others will think of us, because we are worried about protecting our self-images and our sense of identity.

We do not share our deepest thoughts and emotions with one another; we don't acknowledge the feelings of others, or listen to what they really have to say. Most people just wait for the other person to finish talking so that they can state their response. There isn't conversation,

but rather two egos desperate to state their opinion so they can feel validated.

Our society does not operate from the level of consciousness that is needed to sustain seven billion people. We operate on the momentum of an ignorant past, conditioned by generation after generation of unconscious behavior.

It is this conditioning that has caused us to live from the state of consciousness of the ego. It is this conditioning that has caused us to adopt the incorrect view of separation. It is our conditioning that makes us okay with violence, judgment, injustice, and cruelty. It is our conditioning that causes us to act out in unwholesome ways, and seek to benefit ourselves at the expense of others.

From the moment you were born your mind was conditioned by society, molded by the environments that you were put in, shaped by the minds of others who were also conditioned by an ignorant society. You think and act the way you do because it is how you were raised to think and act.

We cannot have peace on Earth if our actions stem from our conditioned minds. We have been conditioned to live according to the standards of a hostile society. In order to have peace, we need to undo our conditioning and retrain our brains to perceive and act in a more harmonious way.

We must unlearn all of the negative habits that we have adopted, and replace them with positive habits, and this can only be done by letting go of everything you have been raised to think, in order to embrace a new reality.

It is difficult to accept that what you thought to be true is actually false, especially if you cling to your beliefs for a sense of identity. But your beliefs are just information stored in your mind, and you are not your mind, and you do not need any thoughts or beliefs about life in order to know your true identity.

To heal the past in you, you have to replace it with presence. We cannot heal our past by thinking about the present with a mind conditioned by the past. As long as we think with our conditioned mind, we will just be recreating the past again and again.

We must replace our conditioned thoughts with our present awareness. We must practice being aware of the thoughts and actions that we think out of habit, and retrain our minds to process life in a more peaceful way.

This practice is known as the practice of "Mindfulness." Mindfulness is the energy of being awake and alert to the present moment. To be mindful means that you are deliberately paying full attention to what is happening around you and within you—in your body, heart, and mind. Mindfulness is awareness without criticism or judgment.

To be mindful of your thoughts means that you can observe your thoughts without labeling or judging them. You let your thoughts come and go as they please, and realize you are not your thoughts. By reducing your attachment to thought, you become less driven by thought, and slowly your conditioned mind begins to fade away as it is replaced with a mind that is present and attentive to life as it is happening now.

Letting go of the past requires that you embrace the present. When you are fully attentive and interested in what is happening in this moment, you have no time to dwell on thoughts of the past or fantasies of the future.

The past and future exist only in your mind. The past is no longer the present, and the future has yet to come. All experiences are experienced in the present moment. The present moment is where life happens. The present moment is life.

Living in the imagined realm of the past or future—the realm of thought that our mind creates and eagerly clings to—only separates us from living in the reality of this moment. The mind tries to grasp the present moment, rather

than letting it be. The mind has no control over the moment and so it fears for its security, since the mind always clings towards comfort; towards what is safe and known.

We can never know the present moment because it is too alive, too vast, too fluid and changing to comprehend. Every moment in time that passes adds an inconceivable amount of new causes and effects to the flow of energy and matter that simply aren't and can't be understood by our brains and their limited sensory perception.

The Universe is a flow that is constantly vibrating, dancing, and changing. We have to go along with the flow of life in order to be at peace. We cannot resist the flow of life and expect to be happy. Resistance to life only makes us suffer.

Allow life to unfold in whatever way that it pleases. You do not need to control anything; everything happens on its own. Remain centered in your awareness where peace is always available. Give up your sense of control and allow the Universe to take its natural course.

In order to heal the past and the conditioned behavior that it has produced, we need to practice being aware of life in this moment. When we are present to life, we have a deep understanding for what needs to be done at each moment in time. We are aware of ourselves and our surroundings, and we are not distracted or separated from life by our overthinking minds.

There is plenty of information about mindfulness and mindfulness practices that you can do, but remember that the words are not the real thing, and reading about mindfulness is not the same as practicing mindfulness for yourself.

To practice mindfulness, you have to be mindful. Meaning you have to be aware of life as it is happening now. Observe this moment without judging it or trying to define it with your mind.

Try sitting silently for a few minutes. Start by breathing slowly and deeply to relax your mind and connect with your body. Then, after a few moments of deep breathing,

see if you can hear or feel your heartbeat. Pay close attention to what is going on inside your body. See if you can feel the billions of cells dancing on your skin, creating a very subtle vibration around your being.

Listen to the sounds in your environment. What noises are appearing in your awareness? What is happening around you? Be aware of this moment and all of the things that are happening in this moment. Can you see how life is happening here and now, and that your thoughts are only separating you from being attentive to life?

See if you can sit silently for a few minutes each day. Just sit and practice being aware of your mind and body. Sit at the back of your mind and observe, be the witness of your thoughts and sensations. Watch the thoughts as they come and go. Where are they coming from? Are you thinking or is thinking happening to you? Can you see how your thoughts appear automatically, without your control? Can you see how they are just a product of the past, a conditioned thought pattern being replayed, as if it were a tape playing an audio recording?

Do you feel any tension in your body that is unnecessary? Are you tensing your eyebrows, lips, or other facial muscles? Are you holding tension in your neck or shoulders? Can you allow your body and mind to simply relax, while you sit there peacefully in your silent awareness?

Can you allow your mind to be just like space? Space allows all things to exist within it, but it is not bound to any of these things. Space lets forms come and go, forever remaining detached from those forms. Can your mind do the same?

Can you allow thought forms to arise without distracting your attention or taking them seriously? Can you allow an angry or sad thought to arise and smile to it, realizing that it is not you who is thinking these thoughts, but that a habitual thought pattern, an energy with great momentum, is simply acting itself out mechanically?

Practice being grounded in your silent awareness. See if you can remain there, and remain aware of whatever is happening in this moment, without trying to cling to what is happening.

Practice it in your daily life. See if you can become aware of the thoughts that arise when you are around others, or when you are in certain situations. What thoughts arise in your mind? What does your mind initially think when someone enters the room? Does your mind judge that person or state some opinion about them? Do you really believe that opinion to be true or even necessary?

Do you worry about the opinion that person might have of you? One of the biggest fears of the ego is the opinion of what others think. This is because the ego needs to uphold the image it has of itself, and if others do not strengthen that image, the ego feels threatened. If you are identified with your self-image, you will always fear what others think of you. But if you realize who you really are, you will not care what people think of you, because you will know who you are, and you will not depend on their opinions for your sense of self-worth.

Someone's perception of you is a reflection of who they are. It has nothing to do with you, so there is no need to take their opinions personally. Respect that they have their own perspective and send them love. People who judge others judge themselves, and that is because they do not know who they really are, and so they depend on judging others in order to strengthen their image of who they are.

You are not your self-image, your ego, or your thoughts. You are the awareness in which these mental forms arise. You are consciousness itself. Only the conditioned mind and the thoughts that it produces can distract you from feeling and living this truth.

Our conditioned mind causes thoughts to arise automatically out of habit. Often these are thoughts that are not peaceful or loving, but are thoughts that were

formed by the ego and its views of separation. The more we can acknowledge these thoughts when they arise, the more capable we are of replacing them with more positive thoughts, or replacing them with our awareness.

The ego and the conditioned mind are acted out unconsciously. If we can make the unconscious conscious, we have already taken the most important step in reconditioning ourselves to live life with more awareness.

Practice being aware of your mind. Try not to be consumed by your mind, and focus more on being present to life as it is happening in this moment. If you are attentive, you will notice that the only time you ever suffer is when you take seriously the thoughts that arise in your mind—when you cling to thought and resist the moment of life happening now, rather than flowing with life and letting nature take its course.

As long as you are living fully attentive to the present moment, and flowing with the current of change, you will be at peace, and will be able to fully engage yourself in whatever presents itself to you.

Practice mindfulness so that you may undo the conditioning that has been done to you, and so that you may be able to live life free of the mind, and free of the conditioning that takes away your peace. Discover the joy that comes from simply being alive, from being present to life, and realizing that you are life, and you are not separate from the environment around you. Mindfulness is the tool that we need to use in order to let go of our limited past, and embrace the infinite realm of possibilities that exist in this moment.

11 Living in Harmony with Nature

When we detach ourselves from our thoughts and our ego, we reconnect to the essence of life that is our true being, and we understand our connection to the Universe and all of its inhabitants. From this understanding of oneness, we can act in a way that benefits all life, because all of our actions will be built on the foundation of respect and appreciation for other living beings.

Our conditioned thoughts produced conditioned actions that were harmful to each other and the planet. Just as we have retrained our minds to process life in a more harmonious way, we need to practice acting and behaving in a more harmonious way. We need to live harmoniously with nature, and take care of nature, so that nature may continue to take care of us.

Nature is not a resource to be mined and used for our benefit. Nature is the producer of life, it is the reason that we are alive, and it deserves to be treated with just as much respect and appreciation as any other thing.

Living in a society that is so disconnected from nature, we fail to realize just how much we depend on nature for survival. We need clean air to breathe and send oxygen to our cells; we cannot continue to use the

inventions that pollute our air and destroy our forests. We need fertile soil to grow our food; we cannot continue to destroy our soil fertility by spraying it with toxic chemicals and pesticides. We need clean water to drink and fuel our bodies; we cannot continue to pollute the water with garbage and fossil fuels.

We need to invent new methods of sustaining ourselves, methods that utilize the abundance of natural energy that the Universe provides. We cannot continue to use these primitive methods of harvesting resources, methods that will inevitably lead to our own destruction if continued.

We need to change our way of life, and transition from a lifestyle based on ignorance and self-benefit, to a lifestyle based on knowledge and love for all beings. You are an essential part of this process. You are existing in the form of a human, meaning that you are not separate from humanity's actions. You have just as much influence over society as anyone else, even if you do not realize it yet.

Society needs to transition from being dependent consumers, to becoming responsible producers. We need to stop draining the earth of its beauty, and instead contribute to it. We need to practice being stewards of the Earth, and taking care of nature and its precious resources.

This means that we need to practice growing our own food, rather than depending on others to produce our food for us. At the very least, we need to at least support companies that practice sustainable production methods, rather than companies that harm the environment.

For every dollar that you spend, you are casting a vote for the kind of world that you want to live in. If you spend money on a product that was produced unsustainably, you are investing in that company and supporting their harmful practices. It may not seem like it, but you have a huge influence over society.

The money that we spend determines the popular markets. If everyone were to buy organic food for example, companies would be forced to match the demand

for organic food, or risk going out of business. It is the same for any market.

The consumers determine the markets, not the producers. If we all demanded that companies practice sustainable methods of production, and stood firm in our demands by only buying products from sustainable producers, all other producers would have to evolve their production methods or risk the collapse of their company.

Voting with your dollar is a very powerful way to determine how things are produced in our society, but it is even more powerful to reduce your need for consumption, and instead produce your own food by respectfully working with the earth.

Humanity needs to return to nature. We live in artificial environments, separated from the earth with concrete, skyscrapers, and roads. Our physical disconnection from nature has produced a spiritual disconnection from nature as well. We no longer see and feel our oneness with the Earth and all of the life that it supports.

In order to restore our connection with nature, we need to live closer to nature, and experience firsthand how nature is our provider; how the Earth is our mother. We cannot proceed to live such unnatural lifestyles and expect this not to have an effect on the Earth.

Reconnecting with nature is a step that humanity must take, but it has to be taken individually, by each one of us. We cannot preach about the need for sustainability yet continue to lead unsustainable lives. No matter how many good thoughts we think, no matter how many good words we say, no matter how good our intentions may be, ultimately our actions determine what is to come of our society.

12 Peace on Earth

Peace on Earth is not a destination, it is a choice that we must make. If humanity as a whole can wake up from our ignorance, realize our oneness, and begin living in harmony with nature and with each other, then peace on Earth can be our reality.

In order for this to happen, we have to cure our ignorant perception of life. We have to see the truth of our existence, and see beyond the views of separation and duality. We have to realize that we are all one, and that our individual actions affect the whole of existence. We have to see clearly our connection to one another, and begin treating one another with kindness, respect, and love.

The current state of society is a result of our current state of being. As a society, we are dominated by our egos and the many fears that stem from a mind identified with ego. Our concern is not for the planet, or for our fellow Earthlings, but for ourselves, for our own lives, and our own experience.

This attitude of self-centered egotism will lead to our destruction if we do not cure it fast. We have already allowed this ignorant perception to produce as much suffering as it has, and it is obvious that if we don't evolve our way of thinking, we will produce our own extinction.

Evolution or extinction. This is the choice that we must make. This is the reality of our situation. Everyone must rise to the occasion and co-create a better society, a

better way of harvesting, managing, and distributing natural resources, a better way of communicating with one another and treating our fellow human beings, a better way of living as humans on this beautiful planet that is our home.

The Earth is suffering, and this suffering needs to stop. But we cannot heal the world without first healing ourselves. We are not separate from the Earth, and the way that we interact with the Earth determines whether the Earth will thrive or deteriorate.

This change is urgent, and the longer we take to evolve our perception, the more destruction our current perception will produce. There is no more room for war, oppression, injustice, slavery, pollution, or destruction. Humanity needs to evolve our way of life, and begin living a life led by love, community, kindness, and stewardship for the Earth. We are responsible for the state of the world, and we are the only ones that can heal the world.

We cannot heal the planet without healing our damaged society, and we cannot heal our damaged society without first healing ourselves. Each of us needs to undo the conditioning that has shaped our behavior, and recondition ourselves to live life in a more peaceful way.

Change will never come from thinking, wishing, or dreaming. Change will come from acting, doing, and living. Change will come when we realize that we have no choice but to evolve our way of life, or produce our own destruction. Change is not a process of staying the same while altering the world around us. Change is a process of personal effort and transformation. Change is something that we need to accomplish within ourselves—within our own minds, our own thoughts, and our own way of behaving with the world. Change is a process of letting go of the past and embracing the present. Real change will only happen when we realize how connected we are to one another, when we realize that "I" and the "other" are not separate, and that we are all in this together. Real change will only come when we awaken from the illusion of separation, and realize our oneness.

"What we now want is closer contact and better understanding between individuals and communities all over the earth, and the elimination of egoism and pride which is always prone to plunge the world into primeval barbarism and strife...
Peace can only come as a natural consequence of universal enlightenment."
– Nikola Tesla

About the Author

Joseph P. Kauffman is the founder of Conscious Collective, LLC—a societally oriented firm that is dedicated to awakening humanity from ignorance and participating in the evolution of human consciousness. Driven by the philosophy of the Bodhisattva, he is passionate about helping others find peace and healing the suffering that exists on this planet.

www.conscious-collective.com

69027077R00047

Made in the USA
Middletown, DE
04 April 2018

CPSIA information can be obtained
at www.ICGtesting.com
Printed in the USA
BVHW051823110922
646759BV00001B/105

9 781956 267716